Paper 1A

Personal Income Tax

ATT
STUDY
TEXT

©
BPP Taxation Courses
1996

**TAXATION
COURSES**

Finance Act 1996 Edition for ATT Qualifying Examinations in November 1996/ May 1997

Published by

BPP Taxation Courses
Faraday House
48 Old Gloucester Street
London
WC1N 3AD

©
BPP Taxation Courses
1996

Printed in England by
DACOSTA PRINT
35/37 Queensland Road
London N7 7AH
(0171) 700 1000

Introduction

Syllabus

The qualifying examination for the Association of Taxation Technicians (ATT) consists of Paper 1 "Personal Taxation" including Professional Responsibilities and Ethics and Paper 2 "Business Taxation", both of three hours' duration. Candidates are also expected to sit papers on "Principles of Law" and "Principles of Accounting", both of one and one-half hours' duration unless they are specifically exempt. Exemptions may be claimed from one, or both these papers by candidates holding a relevant qualification at 'A' Level or above.

The ATT is a body which was established in 1989 under the sponsorship of the Chartered Institute of Taxation (CIoT). It was created so that individuals working in taxation could obtain a recognised professional qualification without necessarily passing the CIoT's Associateship examination.

Our coverage of the Paper 1 syllabus has been split between two study texts:

1A   –   Personal Income Tax (including ethical rules and practice guidelines)

1B   –   Capital Taxes (capital gains tax and inheritance tax).

The Paper 2 syllabus is shown in the Business Income Tax and VAT (2A) study text.

The Paper 1 syllabus is:

"PAPER 1 - PERSONAL TAXATION

This paper covers all aspects of income tax and capital gains tax as they affect individuals, together with a basic knowledge of inheritance tax. You do not need to know about double taxation relief for foreign income.

On income tax you will need to know:

- what is treated as an individual's income for tax purposes and what are the various categories of taxable income including income from land, employment income and benefits in kind, interest and dividend income and foreign income;

- the way in which each type of income is calculated, the "basis of assessment" (that is, the year in which income is taxed) and the various reliefs for expenses incurred and losses;

- the calculation of total income including personal allowances, losses, exemptions and reliefs from tax such as, for example, for charitable payments, pension contributions and payments under the Enterprise Investment Scheme;

- the administration of income tax, including tax returns and the assessment, payment and collection of tax, repayment claims, the deduction of tax at source, the PAYE system for employment income, interest on overdue tax and penalties, and the rights and duties of Inspectors of Taxes and how to appeal against an assessment;

- how married couples and their minor children are taxed.

You will also need to be aware of the Association's practice guidelines and ethical rules relating to dealings with the Revenue departments and the client's tax affairs generally.

On capital gains tax you will need to know:

- when liability to tax may arise;
- what assets are within the scope of the tax;
- how the liability to tax is calculated;
- what exemptions and reliefs are available to individuals;
- the administration of the tax, including tax returns and the assessment of gains, time of payment of tax and the collection of tax, interest on overdue tax and penalties.

For inheritance tax you will be expected to be aware of the implications of lifetime gifts for individuals whether as donors or donees. You will need to know:

- the concept of a transfer of value and the distinction between a chargeable transfer and a potentially exempt transfer;
- how to calculate the tax liability which arises on a chargeable transfer or which may arise on a potentially exempt transfer; and who is responsible for payment of that tax;
- the major exemptions applicable to lifetime transfers;
- the way in which relief may be available on business or agricultural property;
- when property may be related property;
- the principles relating to gifts with reservation."

The Association also publish the following summary of their general examination policy:

1. Questions will not be set which require a knowledge of any statute receiving the Royal Assent or statutory instrument made less than five months before the examination date nor of any legislation repealed or superseded more than five months before the examination date.

2. Questions will not be set which require a knowledge of any case reported less than three months before the examination date.

3. Questions may involve matters which are not listed in the syllabus but which are related to topics within the syllabus (for example, accounting principles for the computation of business income).

4. Questions may involve a knowledge of taxes which are not specifically within the syllabus of a particular paper but which are within the syllabus as a whole.

5. Questions may require candidates to apply tax law and practice to practical problems.

6. Each paper may contain compulsory and optional questions.

7. Candidates should read through the questions carefully before attempting to answer them. The examiners allow time for this when setting the papers.

8. Candidates should attempt the required number of questions in each paper.

It is therefore important that you avoid a narrow-minded approach to the examination, particularly in the case of questions requiring an element of tax planning.

Past ATT examinations

At the time of writing, the published pass rates for recent sittings were:

May 1993	67%
November 1993	54%
May 1994	55%
November 1994	49%
May 1995	56%
November 1995	51%

However, whether an individual candidate passes is dependent largely on the amount and quality of preparation undertaken. The Association state that "students are urged to follow a properly structured course of study specifically designed for the Association's examination" and "most candidates will benefit from following a correspondence course, or from attending evening classes together with, in either case, an intensive revision course immediately before the examination".

It is useful to review the format and content of the previous six Paper 1 examination papers as available at the time of writing:

November 1993 examination

Q1. Written (20 marks)

Basis of Schedule E for UK/non-UK employees.

Q2. Written (20 marks)

Principal private residence.

Q3. Computational (20 marks)

Schedule A profits and losses.

Q4. Computational (20 marks)

Computation of sundry chargeable gains.

Q5. Written (10 marks)

Administration of tax returns, interest and penalties.

Q6. Written (10 marks)

Wasting assets.

Q7. Written (10 marks)

Schedule D IV and V.

Q8. Computational (10 marks)

Retirement relief and gifts relief.

Q9. Computational (10 marks)

Due dates, s.86 interest and repayment supplement.

Q10. Computational (10 marks)

Calculation of benefits in kind.

May 1994 examination

Q1.   Written (20 marks)

The distinction between employment and self-employment.

Q2.   Written (20 marks)

Retirement relief.

Q3.   Computational (20 marks)

Income tax on benefits in kind. Personal pension premiums. Schedule D Case III income.

Q4.   Computational (20 marks)

Capital gains on several assets.

Q5.   Written (10 marks)

The taxation of company cars and fuel.

Q6.   Written (10 marks)

The taxation of termination payments.

Q7.   Written (10 marks)

Determination of UK residence status. The effect of residence on the taxation of income and gains.

Q8.   Computational (10 marks)

Computations of tax repayments.

Q9.   Computational (10 marks)

Interest on tax paid late and repayment supplement.

Q10.   Computational (10 marks)

The gain on a sale of shares.

November 1994 examination

Q1.   Written (20 marks)

Schedule E allowable expenses.

Q2.   Written (20 marks)

Principal private residence relief.

Q3.   Computational (20 marks)

Income tax computation.

Q4.   Computational (20 marks)

Sundry chargeable gains.

Q5.   Written (10 marks)

Appeals, General and Special Commissioners.

Q6.   Written (10 marks)

Pension provisions.

Q7.   Written (10 marks)

Reinvestment relief.

Q8.   Computational (10 marks)

Benefits in kind.

Q9. Computational (10 marks)

Holdover relief for gifts of business assets and retirement relief.

Q10. Computational (10 marks)

Rental income and losses.

May 1995 examination

With effect from May 1995, the ATT taxation papers were re-structured, to comprise 20 compulsory multiple choice questions in Part I and five "traditional" questions in Part II, of which candidates are required to attempt any three. The multiple choice questions account for 40% of the total marks available.

Part I:

Q1. Personal pension premiums computation.

Q2. Additional personal allowance.

Q3. Due dates of payment for Schedule D Case I.

Q4. Beneficial loan for an employee.

Q5. Schedule A profits and losses.

Q6. Basis of assessment – Schedule D Case V.

Q7. Living accommodation benefit in kind.

Q8. Income tax computation.

Q9. Termination payments.

Q10. Opening year losses.

Q11. Disclosure obligations.

Q12. FA 1985 share pool.

Q13. Capital gains and indexation losses.

Q14. Capital gain on pre-1965 unquoted shares.

Q15. Holdover relief and subsequent sale of shares.

Q16. Principal private residence exemption.

Q17. Allowable capital costs for part disposal.

Q18. IHT – gifts and exemptions.

Q19. Due dates of payment for IHT.

Q20. Agricultural property relief.

Part II:

Q1. Schedule E income tax computations.

Q2. Computation of rental income from furnished lettings and furnished holiday lets.

Q3. Advice to client considering retirement in connection with retirement relief and reinvestment relief for CGT purposes.

Q4. Definition of residence and ordinary residence, and the implications for income tax and CGT.

Q5. Detailed rules for self assessment.

Part I:

Q1.   Age relief for PA/MCA.

Q2.   Schedule E 365 day qualifying period.

Q3.   Personal pension premium relief.

Q4.   Schedule E benefit of asset lent/transferred to employee.

Q5.   IT computation with age relief.

Q6.   Schedule E assessment basis for director.

Q7.   Schedule E beneficial loan.

Q8.   Repayment supplement.

Q9.   IT computation with age relief.

Q10. Schedule E car benefits.

Q11. Pay day for CGT assessment under appeal.

Q12. CGT marginal relief for chattels.

Q13. CGT computation for unquoted shares acquired pre-1965.

Q14. Reinvestment relief/retirement relief interaction.

Q15. S.165 hold over relief for a sale at undervalue.

Q16. CGT part disposal calculation.

Q17. PPR/letting relief with periods of non-occupation.

Q18. IHT/BPR on a PET of unquoted shares.

Q19. IHT lifetime exemptions.

Q20. Due date for IHT on a lifetime chargeable transfer.

Part II:

Q1.   Letter on the basic PAYE/NIC procedures for a UK employer.

Q2.   Letter on the CGT/IHT implications of transferring a hotel used partly as a PPR and other lifetime gifts.

Q3.   Income tax computation with Schedule E benefits, relief for trading losses and losses on unquoted shares, dividend and trust income, and EIS relief.

Q4.   Notes on compensation for loss of office, insurance proceeds for damage to an antique and treatment of prize in employee suggestion scheme.

Q5.   CGT computations on sale of shares from FA 1985 and FA 1982 pools, disposal of family company shares with retirement relief, and treatment of losses.

Summary

Note that the "traditional" questions are usually split fairly equally between those requiring a written answer and those which are essentially computational. Although there is a limited element of choice as to which traditional questions to attempt, you must be prepared to tackle both types: the written (letters, reports, memoranda, essays) and the computational. Your studies should therefore be targeted towards this objective.

Naturally, the introduction of multiple choice (or "objective test") questions changes the style of the examination. For the first part of the paper, you will be expected to cover a wide range of topics. Attempting the quiz questions in this text (see below) will be a valuable aspect of preparing for the multiple choice questions. You will also receive as part of your study material a bank of multiple choice questions.

Judicious use of Butterworths Tax Handbooks or similar books produced by CCH Editions, which you can take into the examination hall, can be helpful, but *only if you know where to look* for the information. The books you are allowed to take into the examination may help to remind you of something you know already but had momentarily forgotten. They will not generally help you in answering questions on subjects you know little or nothing about.

About this study text

This study text is divided into sessions and at the end of each session of the text, you will find a *quiz*, comprising a series of short, snappy questions. These questions are designed to test your grasp of certain important principles explained in the preceding chapter.

It is essential that you tackle each quiz as you finish studying a session. Refer back to the text if your answers show that you have not understood any part of the session concerned, before proceeding to the next one.

Solutions to the quiz follow immediately. They are cross-referenced to the session you have just completed.

At the end you will find a bank of *illustrative questions* and suggested solutions. You should attempt each of these questions once you have worked through the relevant session of the study text, and you will be guided to which question to attempt when you have completed the quizzes.

These illustrative questions are designed to provide you with practice in tackling examination-style problems and you should therefore work though the questions carefully *before* checking the suggested solutions. Do not be tempted to "audit" the solution unless and until you have made the best attempt you can. Use Butterworths Tax Handbooks or CCH British Tax Legislation if you need help rather than the study text - this will help you to become familiar with the books which you are allowed to take with you into the examination hall.

For the November 1996 examinations onwards you will not be allowed to take copies of tax tables into the exam room. Instead you will be supplied with a brief set of tables containing all the rates etc. that will be needed. The parts relevant to this study text are shown below:

Extract of tax tables approved for issue in the exam room relevant to personal income tax:

Income tax rates

	1996-97	1995-96
	%	%
Lower rate	20	20
Basic rate	24	25
Higher rate	40	40
Additional rate for trusts	10	10
	£	£
Lower rate band	1-3,900	1-3,200
Basic rate band	3,901-25,500	3,201-24,300

Income tax reliefs

	1996-97	1995-96
	£	£
Personal allowance	3,765	3,525
- age 65-74	4,910	4,630
- age 75 or over	5,090	4,800
Married couple's allowance[1]	1,790	1,720
- age 65-74	3,115	2,995
- age 75 or over	3,155	3,035
Maximum income before abatement of relief	15,200	14,600
Abatement income ceiling		
Single - age 65-74	17,490	16,810
- age 75 or over	17,850	17,150
Married - age 65-74	20,140	19,360
- age 75 or over	20,580	19,780
Additional allowance for children[1]	1,790	1,720
Widow's bereavement allowance[1]	1,790	1,720
Mortgage interest: loan limit[1]	30,000	30,000
'Rent-a-room' limit	3,250	3,250

Note:
[1] relief is restricted to 15%.

Income tax - pension contributions

Personal pension premiums		Retirement annuity premiums	
Age	%	Age	%
Up to 35	17.5		
36-45	20		
46-50	25	Up to 50	17.5
51-55	30	51-55	20.0
56-60	35	65-60	22.5
61 or over	40	61 or over	27.5

Age is taken at the start of the fiscal year

PPS earnings cap	1996-97 - £82,200
	1995-96 - £78,600

Company cars and fuel

Cash equivalent is 35% of list price, reduced by one-third if the car is more than 4 years old at the end of the fiscal year.

Further reductions: business miles > 2,500 - one third
                                      > 18,000 - two thirds

Full scale benefit - income tax, VAT, National Insurance

	Petrol		Diesel	
	1996-97	1995-96	1996-97	1995-96
Up to 1400cc	£710	£670	£640	£605
1401-2000cc	£890	£850	£640	£605
Over 2000cc	£1,320	£1,260	£820	£780

Fixed Profit car scheme rates

	1996-97		1995-96	
Engine size	First 4000 business miles	Additional business miles	First 4000 business miles	Additional business miles
Up to 1000cc	27p	16p	27p	15p
1001cc-1500cc	34p	19p	34p	19p
1501cc-2000cc	43p	23p	43p	23p
2001cc or over	61p	33p	60p	32p

National Insurance Contributions

	1996-97	1995-96

Class 1 contributions

Lower earnings limit £3,172 (£61/week) £3,016 (£58/week)
Upper earnings limit £23,660 (£455/week) £22,880 (£440/week)

Employees' contributions: 2% on lower earnings limit plus 10% (8.2% if contracted out) on excess earnings, up to the upper earnings limit.

Class 2 contributions

Normal rate	£6.05 pw	£5.75 pw
Small earnings exception	£3,430 pa	£3,260 pa

Class 3 contributions £5.95 pw £5.65 pw

Class 4 contributions

Percentage rate	6%	7.3%
Annual lower earnings limit	£6,860	£6,640
Annual upper earnings limit	£23,660	£22,880

There is a *comprehensive index* at the very back of this study text.

You will find that certain paragraphs have been highlighted (for example, as this paragraph). This is where the text has been changed substantially from the FA 1995 edition. If you have already started studying using the FA 1995 study text, you may prefer to read only the highlighted paragraphs. Most examples have been updated by one year and some new examples have been inserted. As question practice is vital, we would recommend that you rework all examples and quiz questions. Where a large block of text is new, we have highlighted a note at the start of the block, rather than highlighting pages of text. Some text has been re-written, but says the same as the previous text in different words. Such text has not been highlighted.

Personal income tax
Contents

SESSION 1
OUTLINE OF UK INCOME TAX

The purpose of this session is to:

- identify the main taxes levied in the UK
- identify the sources of tax law
- explain the role of the Inland Revenue
- identify the groups of taxpayers liable to income tax

References ICTA 1988 unless other wise stated

1.1 Introduction

1.1.1 Taxes levied in the UK

In the UK, central government raises over £170 billion (that is, one hundred and seventy thousand million pounds) in taxation each year. The split is, roughly:

(a)	income tax	27%
(b)	national insurance	20%
(c)	corporation tax	13%
(d)	capital gains tax, inheritance tax and stamp duty	4%
(e)	value added tax	18%
(f)	customs duty, tobacco, petrol and other expenditure taxes	18%

Items (a), (b) (c) and (d) are sometimes known as direct taxes. Items (e) and (f) are indirect taxes. The distinction is simply that in the case of direct taxes the revenue authority collects directly (and we must count the PAYE system as a form of direct collection) from the taxpayer, whereas in the case of indirect taxes the revenue authority collects from an intermediary, who attempts to pass on the cost to the final consumer.

There are other classifications which may be helpful. Items (a) (b) and (c) are, in general, taxes on income whereas those under (d) are sometimes known as capital taxes. The indirect taxes in (e) and (f) are sometimes called expenditure taxes.

1.2 Tax law

1.2.1 Sources of law

Tax law is made by statute - though it is interpreted and amplified by case law. The main taxes, their incidence and their sources, are set out in the table below.

Tax	Suffered by	Source
Income tax	Individuals Partnerships Trusts Personal representatives	Income and Corporation Taxes Act (ICTA 1988) as amended by subsequent Finance Acts
Corporation tax	Companies	As above
Capital gains tax	Individuals Trusts Personal representatives Companies (which pay tax on capital gains in the form of corporation tax)	Taxation of Chargeable Gains Act 1992 (TCGA 1992) as amended
Value added tax	Businesses, both in- corporated and unin- corporated	Value Added Tax Act 1994 (VATA 1994) as amended
Inheritance tax	Individuals Trusts	Inheritance Tax Act (IHTA 1984) as amended

1.2.2 The legislative process

The *tax year*, or *fiscal year*, or *year of assessment* runs from 6 April to 5 April following. For example, the year of assessment of 1996/97 runs from 6 April 1996 to 5 April 1997.

Finance Acts make changes which apply mainly to the tax year ahead. For example, the Finance Act 1996 is concerned with the tax year 1996/97 for income tax purposes. This study text sets out the law as it stands in relation to the tax year 1996/97, including the provisions of the Finance Act 1996 which students taking exams in November 1996 and May 1997 will be expected to know.

The annual Budget process commences each November with the Chancellor presenting a Budget speech announcing, amongst other things, the changes to taxation proposed for the coming fiscal year. A Finance Bill is printed early in the New Year and, after Parliamentary debate and various amendments, passes into law (by receiving Royal Assent to become a Finance Act) some time before 5 May.

Most income tax law has been consolidated; in 1990 into CAA 1990 - The Capital Allowances Act; in 1988 into ICTA 1988 - The Income and Corporation Taxes Act; and in 1970 into TMA 1970 - The Taxes Management Act. The Taxes Management Act provides the Inland Revenue's authority and the framework for administering the income tax system. Other provisions are found in subsequent Finance Acts. The consolidation acts are amended by the annual Finance Act which broadly enacts the Budget proposals.

Statutory Instruments (SI) are used by the Government as a convenient way of introducing detailed legislation. For example, s.203 ICTA 1988 empowers the Board of Inland Revenue to make regulations by statutory instrument on a range of administrative matters for operating PAYE on employment income. An 'instrument' is laid before Parliament and, unless objection is made to it, it normally becomes law within a stated time limit. Statutory Instruments are numbered on a calendar year basis (eg. SI 1995/493 is SI No. 493 issued in 1995).

The Treasury is required each year around Budget time to update various tax related allowances (eg. personal allowances), bands and exemptions in line with the movement in the Retail Prices Index (RPI) by laying a series of SIs before Parliament. However, it is common for most of these changes to be over ridden by the Chancellor.

1.3   The Inland Revenue

1.3.1   Organisation of the Inland Revenue

It is helpful to set out in diagrammatic form the system in operation for the administration of income tax in the UK.

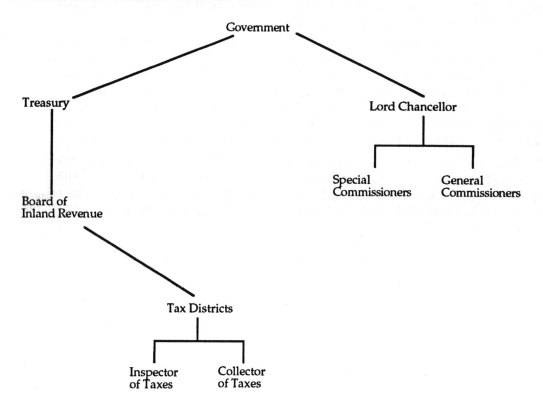

The *Treasury* is the ministry concerned with the imposition and collection of taxation. The day to day management of the Treasury is the responsibility of the Chancellor of the Exchequer. The Treasury appoint the *Board of the Inland Revenue* (also known as the *Commissioners of Inland Revenue*), a body of civil servants. The Board administers the system of direct taxation in the UK (not only income tax but corporation tax, capital gains tax, stamp duties and inheritance tax). The various provisions relating to the administration of direct taxes in the UK are contained in the *Taxes Management Act 1970 (TMA 1970)*.

For the purposes of administration of income tax, the UK is divided into a number of *regions* (each under a regional controller) and each region is subdivided into *districts* (although some specialist offices - eg. the pension schemes office (PSO) dealing with pensions - also exist). Each district has a *district inspector* in charge and he is assisted by other inspectors and clerical staff. The official title for an inspector is *HM Inspector of Taxes* (HMIT). The main work of the districts conducted through local tax offices consists of examining the returns and accounts of individuals, businesses and companies and the computation of the amount of tax due. They also notify the taxpayer of the tax that is due by sending to him or *'raising' a notice of assessment.*

The *collection* of tax that is due is *not* the responsibility of the inspectors but of the *collectors of taxes*. These are civil servants appointed by the Board of Inland Revenue. The collection of tax has, until now, been kept *quite separate* from its assessment. If tax which is due is not paid, the collector will pursue the debt through the courts; small amounts (less than £2,000) being pursued through the magistrates' courts, and larger amounts through the county or high courts. In extreme circumstances, the collector may seize the assets of the taxpayer.

TMA 1970 ss.65 & 66

There are plans to combine the inspector and collector functions and for local tax offices and collection offices to be restructured into new-style taxpayer service offices and taxpayer district offices. The taxpayer service offices will perform the day to day work on PAYE codes, changes to personal reliefs, assessments, and initiating collection while the taxpayer district offices will conduct compliance work, such as examination of selected business accounts, PAYE audit, and follow up collection work. In some locations a taxpayer assistance office will produce a counter service for personal callers requiring forms or leaflets or answers to basic queries.

A number of changes are being made to accommodate the introduction of self-assessment due for individuals from 1996/97. For example the assessment and collection functions will merge with Inspectors and Collectors to be known as 'officers of the Board'. Self-assessment will not require the issuing of an assessment in its present form.

1.3.2   The Commissioners

The General Commissioners are appointed by the Lord Chancellor to hear appeals (see below) against assessments issued by the inspector. They are part-time and unpaid apart from travelling and subsistence expenses and are chosen from business and professional people. They are appointed for a local area (a *division*). They appoint a clerk who is often a lawyer or accountant and who is paid for his services by the Board of the Inland Revenue.

TMA 1970 ss.2 & 3

The Special Commissioners are also appointed by the Lord Chancellor. They operate from London but go *'on circuit'* around the provinces during the year. They are full-time paid professionals who must be barristers, advocates or solicitors of not less than 10 years' standing. They generally hear appeals involving more complex points and areas of the legislation.

TMA 1970 s.4

1.3.3   Inland Revenue pronouncements

The Inland Revenue issue booklets available to the general public on a range of matters (eg. IR20 on the foreign element of taxation). They represent the Revenue's understanding of the law but are not binding on the taxpayer. The Revenue also issue dated press releases on a variety of matters, sometimes to announce intended legislative changes which will subsequently take effect from the date of the press release.

The Revenue also publish 'Revenue Interpretations' and other explanatory material in their magazine *Tax Bulletin*. From 1995 their own internal guidance material, the Inspectors' manuals, is available either for sale to the public in various different forms including CD-ROM or for inspection at any tax office.

Where the Revenue wish to publish a note on the way they deal with a practical area, they may issue a Statement of Practice (eg. SP 1/96 is the first SP issued in 1996).

Occasionally, the Revenue decide to mitigate the effect of legislation, generally either because it is fair to the taxpayer to do so or it is unduly inconvenient to the Revenue to apply it rigorously. In that case they issue an extra-statutory concession (ESC). Taxpayers could be denied the benefits of a particular ESC if they have deliberately set out to save tax by manipulating the ESC. This case concerns Capital Gains Tax but the principle established applies to all taxes. Details of the case are given in the Capital Gains Tax part of the Capital Taxes study text, at 1.6.1.

R v IRC ex parte Fulford-Dobson, 1987

1.3.4   The tax practitioner as agent of the taxpayer

In this chapter we have spoken of the taxpayer, the person who suffers tax. In practice, of course, many taxpayers arrange for their tax practitioners to prepare and submit their tax returns. But it is important to realise that the taxpayer is still the person *responsible* for submitting that return and for paying whatever tax becomes due - the tax practitioner is only acting as the taxpayer's *agent*, and as such cannot take over the taxpayer's duties and responsibilities. Contractual obligations and professional requirements should however ensure that the tax practitioner performs competently. These matters are covered in a separate study text.

1.4 Incidence of income tax

1.4.1 General

The following may be liable to income tax:

(a)   men and women;

(b)   children, however young;

(c)   trustees, in respect of trust income;

(d)   personal representatives, in respect of income accruing to the estate of a deceased person; and

(e)   partnerships (but not after 1996/97 as each partner will be treated as carrying on a separate business for tax purposes).

NB: It should be noted that whilst companies pay corporation tax, many of the income tax rules will be applied in calculating the amount of profits chargeable to corporation tax.

1.4.2 Children

The personal allowance (PA), which is £3,765 for 1996/97 and which is available to all UK or EEA (European Economic Area) resident individuals, acts as a threshold for taxable income so that, in practice, most children will have no tax liability on any earnings or investment income that they may enjoy during a tax year. In fact, by virtue of the personal allowance, some children are able to claim a repayment of tax suffered at source on investment income. The effect of the PA is such that the first £3,765 of income in a tax year is tax-free.

There is an important exception to the proposition that a child is a taxpayer in his own right. Investment income of a child, unmarried and under 18, which arises out of a gift, covenant, settlement or other disposition made by his parent is treated as (and aggregated with) the income of that parent, provided that it exceeds £100 pa. Income attributed to the parent under this provision is taxed under Schedule D Case VI.

s.660B

s.660C

1.4.3 Husband and wife

Married men and women are taxable persons in their own right each with their own personal allowances and bands of tax (first £3,900 at 20%, next £21,600 at 24%, and the balance at 40% for 1996/97). A husband is, however also entitled to a married couple's allowance (MCA), which reduces his tax by 15% of the allowance and is £1,790 for 1996/97. One half of the MCA can be claimed by the wife and, if a joint election is made, all the MCA can be allocated to the wife. One spouse can elect to surrender any surplus MCA to the other spouse.

If one spouse has unused allowances there is scope to save tax by arranging for income-bearing assets to pass from one spouse to the other. Similarly if spouses pay tax at different rates a transfer of income should be considered. A gift of income bearing assets between spouses must be "without strings attached" otherwise the income remains that of the original owner. This topic is covered in detail in Session 2.

1.4.4 Residence, ordinary residence, domicile

A taxpayer may be:

(a)   resident; and/or

(b)   ordinarily resident; and/or

(c)   domiciled (ie. permanently resident)

in the UK. If he was born in the UK of UK domiciled parents and has never left the UK for any length of time he is likely to be all three. Another individual may be non-resident or non-ordinarily resident or non-domiciled. Various combinations are possible and depend on the facts of each case as well as legislation and Revenue practice.

Later in this text - in session 8.1 - we set out the definitions of residence, ordinary residence and domicile.

At this stage in the text it is sufficient to consider the broad principles determining which persons are assessed to UK tax and whether the tax applies just to their UK income or to income from overseas as well.

Generally, a UK resident person is liable to UK income tax on his UK *and* foreign income whereas a non-resident is liable to UK income tax only on income *arising* in the UK. If non-residents were treated identically to UK residents the UK Inland Revenue would try to collect income tax from French residents on their French income. You can imagine the consequences!

A UK resident, who is not domiciled in the UK, however, is liable to UK tax on foreign income on a *remittance* basis only - ie. only to the extent that such income is brought to the UK.   s.65(4)

The remittance basis for foreign income also applies to Commonwealth and Irish citizens resident but not ordinarily resident in the UK.

Interest on many UK government securities is exempt from UK income tax if the recipient is not ordinarily resident in the UK. The securities include $3^{1}/_{2}$% War Loan, all issues of Funding Loan and most issues of Treasury Stock and Exchequer Loan. UK bank deposit or building society interest received gross is also treated in a similar manner.   s.47

s.128 FA 1995

1.4.5 Exempt persons

To conclude this section, here is an abbreviated list of persons or bodies exempt from UK income tax:

(a)   representatives of foreign countries;

(b)   visiting members of foreign armed services to the extent of their service pay only;

(c)   approved pension funds;

(d)   UK registered charities;

(e)   friendly societies;

(f)   trade unions.

QUESTIONS

1. A "fiscal year" is a 12 month period running from 1 April to the following 31 March. TRUE/FALSE?

2. What is the "Board of Inland Revenue"?

3. What are the functions of an inspector of taxes?

4. Both the General Commissioners and the Special Commissioners exercise a judicial role in hearing appeals by taxpayers against assessments to tax. TRUE/FALSE?

5. Distinguish between the General Commissioners and the Special Commissioners.

6. The income of a minor child (aged less than 18) is always treated as income of his parent. TRUE/FALSE?

7. To what extent are the following individuals liable to UK income tax?

    (a) John Smith, resident, ordinarily resident and domiciled in UK, who has both UK and foreign source income.

    (b) Johann Schmidt, who has never been to the UK, but who receives rental income from a property in London in addition to his salary from his German employer. Johann has always lived in Germany.

SOLUTIONS

1.   FALSE - it runs from 6 April to the following 5 April (1.2.2).

2.   A body of civil servants, responsible for administering the system of direct taxation in the UK (1.3.1).

3.   (a)   Examining returns and accounts submitted by taxpayers;

     (b)   Computing the resultant liabilities to tax;

     (c)   Issuing notices of assessment to taxpayers, indicating the amount of tax due.
     (1.3.1)

4.   TRUE (1.3.2).

5.   *General Commissioners*: part-time; paid expenses only; not necessarily legal (or tax) experts.

     Special Commissioners: full-time; salaried; must be barristers, advocates or solicitors of at least 10 years' standing.
     (1.3.2)

6.   FALSE - the income is only treated as the parent's income (broadly) if it is derived from the parent and exceeds £100 in the year of assessment (1.4.2).

7.   (a)   John Smith is liable to UK income tax on all his income, regardless of where it arises.

     (b)   Johann Schmidt, being not resident in the UK, is liable to UK income tax only in respect of income arising in UK, ie. on his UK rental income.
     (1.4.4)

SESSION 2

TAXABLE INCOME

The purpose of this session is to:

- explain how income from all sources is aggregated in order to compute an individual's liability to income tax

- identify the distinction between assessed income and income taxed at source

- outline the categories of assessed income by Schedule and Case, indicating the type of income taxed by each

- explain the nature of charges on income and the payments which qualify as such

- identify the allowances available to taxpayers as deductions from their total income

- identify the tax reducers available to individuals

- describe and illustrate a total income computation

- describe the special rules that apply in taxing savings income

- explain the mechanics of tax relief on retainable charges and assessments when retainable charges exceed total income

- set out the tax position of husbands, wives and children

References to ICTA 1988 unless otherwise stated.

2.1 Aggregation of Income

An individual's income from all sources is brought together in a *personal tax computation*. Here is an example.

A TAXPAYER: INCOME TAX COMPUTATION 1996/97	£
Assessed income (gross)	36,000
Income taxed at source (gross)	5,000
	41,000
Less charges on income (gross)	(2,000)
Statutory total income (STI)	39,000
Less personal allowance	(3,765)
Taxable income	**£35,235**

Income tax	£	£
£3,900 x 20%		780
£21,600 x 24%		5,184
£9,735 x 40%		3,894
		9,858
Less tax reducer		
Married couple's allowance £1,790 x 15%		(269)
Tax borne		9,589
Add basic rate tax withheld on charges		
Paid net £2,000 x 24%		480
Tax payable		10,069
Less tax suffered		
PAYE tax on salary (assessed income) (say)	8,250	
Lower rate tax on income taxed at source		
£5,000 x 20%	1,000	
		(9,250)
Tax due under self-assessment		£819

The figures for *statutory total income (STI)* and *taxable income* are both important, as we shall see.

Charges are deductible in arriving at STI. Charges include payments made by the taxpayer under a deed of covenant to a charity or as a one-off 'gift aid' payment. Other examples of charges are patent royalties and interest paid on loans for a qualifying purpose but not on loans to acquire one's home.

The personal allowance (currently £3,765) is then deducted to arrive at taxable income.

In the computation of income tax note also the three figures: tax borne (the burden of tax), tax payable (the amount which must be accounted for to the Inland Revenue) and tax due under self-assessment (the balance of the liability still to be settled in cash - see Session 3).

Income tax is charged on the figure of 'taxable income', on the first £3,900 at the lower rate (20%), on the next £21,600 at the basic rate (24%) and on any excess at the higher rate (40%). Any tax already suffered by deduction at source is given as a credit against the tax payable. Most forms of savings income such as interest and dividends are received net of 20% tax.

s.1

The layout above indicates the principles used to establish an individual's liability to income tax. The remainder of this session gives more details of this computation.

2.2 Direct assessment and tax at source

2.2.1 Introduction

Some income is received in full, with no tax deducted in advance. This income is then taxed by the inspector sending out (*raising*) an assessment. This is *income taxed by direct assessment*. Such income received gross will be 'self-assessed' under the new self assessment regime for 1996/97 onwards.

Other income is received after deduction of basic rate tax (24%) or lower rate tax (20%). This is *income taxed at source*. An assessment is then only needed if the recipient is liable to higher rate tax (40%). If the recipient is not liable to tax at all, a repayment of the 24%/20% tax deducted is due. If the income is taxable at the lower rate (20%), a partial repayment is due if it has suffered tax at 24% at source.

The taxable income for a tax year (6 April in one year to 5 April in the next) is the *gross* amount (that is, adding back any tax deducted at source) and is in many cases the income arising in that year. But an important rule about some kinds of income taxed by direct assessment was that the income to be assessed in a tax year was not the income arising in that tax year but the income of some previous period: the *preceding year basis* (PYB). Notwithstanding the new current year basis rules (see 5.1.5) the PYB continued to apply until 1995/96 for some sources of investment income existing before 6 April 1994. For such sources, 1996/97 is a 'transitional year' for which the assessment is half the income arising in 1995/96 and 1996/97.

2.2.2 The Schedular system

Each of the types of income taxed by direct assessment or, for 1996/97 onwards, by self-assessment, is taxed under a set of rules known as a Schedule. Schedules D and E are divided into Cases.

ss.15 - 20

Schedule A   Income from all types of land and buildings is assessed as a 'Schedule A Business'. (Note this approach applies for individuals but not for companies.)

Schedule D

Case I	Profits of trades
Case II	Profits of professions or vocations
Case III	Interest received *without* deduction of tax at source
Case IV	Interest on foreign securities (such as debentures)
Case V	Income from foreign possessions (for example foreign dividends, rents, business profits and pensions)
Case VI	Any annual profits not falling under any other Schedule or Case (such as casual commissions)

Schedule E   Income from an office or employment including salaries, bonuses, benefits in kind and pensions (including certain annuities, but not any pension from outside the UK). The assessment is on the actual income paid *in* the tax year, and most tax is collected under the PAYE system. Despite the collection of tax before the employee receives the money, this income still counts as assessed income and not as income taxed at source. The cases of Schedule E relate to the residence/domicile status of the employee and the country of employment

Schedules B and C have been abolished.

Schedule F does not apply to individual taxpayers, but to UK companies paying dividends. The recipients of such income are taxed under rules which are separate from the Schedular system. The advance corporation tax paid by a company to the Revenue when paying a dividend is imputed to the shareholder as though it were income tax; therefore no formal assessment under Schedule F is necessary.

The types of income which may for the time being continue to be assessed on a preceding year basis (PYB) are those within the first five cases of Schedule D. Without exception these sources will all be taxable on a current year basis with effect from 1997/98.

The schedules and cases are important because each has its own set of rules, including (up to 1995/96) those relating to the date of payment of tax. Once we have decided that income should be assessed (or self-assessed) under, say, Schedule A, the rules of Schedule A determine the amount of income. Each of the types of income is considered in detail later in this text.

The work of the Revenue is often fragmented by reference to schedules. Each district office has at least a Schedule D and a Schedule E department which operate separately. Indeed, rather than being issued with a total assessment a taxpayer may receive a Schedule D assessment only or a Schedule E assessment only. Of course, the tax due will be based on a computation of all income.

This fragmented approach to tax liability is removed by self-assessment with individual tax payers computing a single liability in one exercise, albeit payable in three amounts (see Session 3).

2.2.3 Income taxed at source

The following income is received net of tax at the lower rate.

(a)   Interest on most government stocks

(b)   Interest paid by UK companies on debentures and loan stocks

(c)   Building society interest paid to individuals

(d)   Bank deposit interest paid to individuals

(e)   The income portion of a purchased annuity

UK dividends are also treated as if received net of lower rate tax although, strictly, the amount received has a tax credit 'imputed' to it with the paying company accounting for tax at 20/80 of the dividend declared (ie. paid).

Patent royalties are received net of basic rate tax. Copyright royalties are received gross.

In examinations you may be given either the net or the gross amount of such income: read the question carefully. If you are given the net amount (the amount received or credited), you should gross up the figure at the rate of 20%. For example, if Jack Sprat receives net building society interest of £160 it is equivalent to gross income of:

	Income	Tax at source
£160 x 100/80	£200	£40*

* ie. £200 x 20%

If a recipient is not liable to tax, he can recover the lower rate tax suffered, or, in respect of bank or building society interest, he can certify in advance that he is a non-taxpayer and be paid the interest gross. If he so certifies himself but turns out to be liable to tax after all, the interest is taxable (under Schedule D Case III) as income of the year of receipt.

A non-taxpayer cannot arrange in advance to receive dividends gross, but he can get the 20/80 tax credit imputed repaid to him.

2.3 Layout of personal tax computations

The whole of this section has been substantially rewritten.

2.3.1 Savings income and other income

A distinction is made between savings and other income. Savings income comprises:

(a) Interest (including interest from banks, building societies, gifts, debentures and the National Savings Bank)

(b) Dividends

(c) The income part of a purchased life annuity

(d) Equivalent foreign income not taxed on the remittance basis

Charges and allowances are set against other income in priority to savings income.

2.3.2 Typical Personal tax computation

Here is a typical personal tax computation. Note the way in which it is set out. Later sessions expand on the points arising in the example.

MR TAXPAYER: INCOME TAX COMPUTATION 1996/97

	Other Income £	Savings Income £	Tax Suffered £
Schedule D Case I business profit	23,950		
Less: personal pension contribution	(1,080)		
	22,870		
Schedule A rental income	2,000		
Dividends £4,348 x $^{100}/_{80}$		5,435	1,087
Bank deposit interest £1,200 x $^{100}/_{80}$		1,500	300
Building Society interest £288 x $^{100}/_{80}$		360	72
Less: charge on income paid covenanted payment to charity £76 x $^{100}/_{76}$	(100)		
STI (total £32,065)	24,770	7,295	
Less: personal allowance	(3,765)		
Taxable income (total £28,300)	£21,005	£7,295	
Tax suffered at source			£1,459

Income tax		£		£
Lower rate band		3,900	x 20%	780
Basic rate band	other income £(21,005 - 3,900)	17,105	x 24%	4,105
	savings income £(25,500 - 21,005)	4,495	x 20%	899
Higher rate	£(7,295 - 4,495)	2,800	x 40%	1,120
		£28,300		6,904
Less: tax reducer				
married couple's allowance (£1,790 x 15%)				(269)
Tax borne				6,635
Add: tax retained on charge paid net				
(£100 x 24%)				24
Tax payable				6,659
Less: tax deducted at source				(1,459)
Tax due under self-assessment				£5,200

Note that the basic rate band is split into two parts: savings income and other income. Savings income is treated as the top slice of a taxpayer's income, in this case the £2,800 taxable at 40% plus the £4,495 in the basic rate band.

There are two exceptions to the rule that savings income is treated as the top slice of a taxpayer's income. The taxable part of partially exempt payments on the termination of employment and taxable gains on life assurance policies are both put into income above savings income, so that a taxpayer with £20,000 of salary, £10,000 of bank interest and a £100,000 termination payment would still have some bank interest within the basic rate band (and therefore taxable at only 20%) and some within the 40% band.

s.207A(3)

2.3.3 Repayment claim

The layout for a repayment claim is similar to an ordinary income tax computation.

MR D: INCOME TAX REPAYMENT CLAIM 1996/97

	Other Income £	Savings income £	Tax suffered £
Schedule E salary (taxed under PAYE)	4,005		101
Less: deductible expenses	(70)		
	3,935		
Schedule A	100		
Building society interest £160 x 100/80		200	40
Less: charges paid gross (against other income first)	(250)	(200)	
STI	3,785	nil	
Less: personal allowance	(3,765)		
Taxable income	£20	nil	
Tax suffered at source			141
Tax borne £20 x 20%			(4)
Tax repayable			£137

2.3.4 Payments out of funds not charged to income tax

If charges paid net exceed total income (ignoring charges) minus allowances deductible from STI, an assessment will be made on the payer for the basic rate tax he has deducted, under s.350 ICTA 1988. In other words, the Revenue ensures that you do not get tax relief for charges if you are not a payer of tax.

s.350

Example

For 1996/97 B, a single person, has earnings of £3,800 and pays a deed of covenant to a charity of £1,000 (the gross amount). What is his tax payable?

Solution

	£
Income	3,800
Less: charge	(1,000)
STI	2,800
Less: personal allowance	(3,765)
Taxable income	nil

	£
Tax borne	nil
Add: tax retained on charge £1,000 x 24%	240
Tax payable	£240

The tax payable can be analysed as follows.

	£
Tax on charge relieved against income £(3,800 - 3,765) = £35 x 24%	8
Tax on charge not paid out of income £(1,000 - 35) = £965 x 24%	232
	£240

Example

Jackie, a married woman whose husband has no income, has the following income and outgoings for 1996/97.

	£
Salary (tax deducted under PAYE £4,000)	25,000
Building society interest received (net)	5,000
Mortgage interest paid under MIRAS (net amount)	1,140
Qualifying charitable donations paid under gift-aid (gross amount)	800

What is Jackie's tax payable for 1996/97?

Solution

	Other income	Savings income	Tax suffered
	£	£	£
Schedule E	25,000		4,000
Building Society interest			
£ 5,000 x $^{100}/_{80}$		6,250	1,250
Less: charge	(800)		
STI (total £30,450)	24,200	6,250	
Less: PA	(3,765)		
Taxable income (total £26,685)	£20,435	£6,250	
Tax suffered			£5,250

Income tax

Lower rate band	3,900	x 20%	780
Basic rate band other income £(20,435 - 3,900)	16,535	x 24%	3,968
savings income £(25,500 - 20,435)	5,065	x 20%	1,013
Higher rate £(6,250 - 5,065)	1,185	x 40%	474
	£26,685		6,235

Less: tax reducer:	
MCA transferred from husband £1,790 x 15%	(269)
Tax borne	5,966
Add: basic rate tax retained on charge (£800 x 24%)	192
Tax payable	6,158
Less: tax suffered	(5,250)
Tax due under self-assessment	£908

Notes:

(a)   Mortgage interest qualifies for relief at 15%. If it is paid under the MIRAS (mortgage interest relief at source) scheme relief is obtained automatically by only paying 85% of the amount due to the lender. MIRAS payments can therefore be totally ignored for the tax computation.

(b)   Tax relief was obtained on the charitable donation by retaining 24% (£192). However, the gross amount of £800 is fully deducted giving tax relief at the marginal rate of 40%. As this is 24% too much relief in total the tax retained on the charge is clawed back to arrive at tax payable.

(c)   In fact the charge actually saves tax at 44% in the computation - at 40% by reducing income in the higher rate band and at 4% by shifting income qualifying at the 20% rate into the 24% band. This 4% bonus is not clawed back.

2.4 Charges on income

2.4.1 Introduction

The layout in sections 2.1 and 2.3 above shows a deduction for *charges on income*. A charge on income is a payment by the taxpayer which income tax law allows as a deduction in arriving at Statutory Total Income (STI).

The only types of payment to be treated as charges are those which are:

s.347A

(a)   Covenanted payments and one off 'gift-aid' charitable gifts

(b)   Payments of eligible interest

(c)   Certain payments made for proper commercial reasons in connection with the individual's trade, profession or vocation

(d)   Certain payments for vocational training

Charges on income fall into two categories: those from which basic rate income tax is first deducted by the payer (charges paid *net* - also referred to as 'retainable' charges) and those which are paid without any deduction (charges paid *gross* - referred to as 'non-retainable' charges) It is always the *gross* figure which is shown as a deduction in the payer's tax computation.

The following are the major categories of charges on income which are paid net of basic rate tax.

s.349

(a)   Payments to charities under deed of covenant and one-off charitable gifts

(b)   Royalties on patents

(c)   Certain expenditure by an individual on vocational training

The recipient of a payment from which basic rate income tax has been deducted is treated as having paid that amount of tax in advance. If the tax deducted exceeds his actual liability, he may claim a repayment from the Revenue.

The remaining types of charges on income are paid gross. These include:

(a)   Eligible interest

(b)   Copyright royalties

2.4.2 Deeds of covenant

A deed of covenant is a legally enforceable agreement by which the payer agrees to make payments without receiving consideration in return.

s.347A(2)

Tax relief, as a charge on income, is available to the payer of a deed of covenant *to a charity*, provided that all the following conditions are fulfilled.

(a)   The covenant is capable of exceeding three years

s.347A(7)

(b)   The deed cannot be revoked at the payer's option within the first three years

(c)   The deed was not made for consideration in money or money's worth

Covenants are often used as a means of paying subscriptions to charities that offer free or reduced rate rights of admission (as with the National Trust). Where this benefit is offered, it does not infringe the general rule that a covenant must not have been made for a consideration in money or money's worth, so long as the charity's sole or main purpose is the preservation of property or the conservation of wildlife.

2.4.3 One-off charitable gifts

One-off charitable gifts (of money only) by individuals qualify for tax relief as charges under the gift aid scheme provided the gifts are each for £250 net (£329 gross) or more and are made under deduction of basic rate tax.

s.25 FA 1990

The gift must not be subject to any condition for repayment, and the total benefits received in the tax year by the donor and any persons connected with him from the charity must not be worth more than the lower of (i) 2.5% of the net gift and (ii) £250.

2.4.4 Eligible interest

Interest on a loan is a charge when the loan is used for one of the following qualifying purposes.

Note that the purchase of the borrower's own residence is *not* a qualifying purpose. The tax treatment of such loans is explained in section 2.6 below.

s.353

(a)   The purchase of an interest in a partnership, or contribution to the partnership of capital or a loan. The borrower must be a partner (other than a limited partner), and relief ceases when he ceases to be one.

s.362(1)

(b)   The purchase of ordinary shares in a close company (other than a close investment holding company) or the loan of money to such a company for use in its business, provided that when the interest is paid the individual either has (with any associates) a material (more than 5%) interest in the close company, or holds (ignoring associates) *some* ordinary share capital and works full time as a manager or director of the company.

s.360(1)

If, however, the company exists wholly or mainly for the purpose of holding investments or other property and any property held by the company is used as a residence by the borrower then the borrower must work for the greater part of his time in the business. A close company is (broadly) a company controlled by its shareholder-directors or by five or fewer shareholders. Relief for interest is not available if relief for the investment is claimed under the enterprise investment scheme (see Session 5).

(c)   Investment in a co-operative. This provision applies to investment in shares or through loans to the co-operative. The borrower must work for the greater part of his time in the co-operative.

s.361(1)

(d)   The purchase of shares in an employee-controlled company. The company must be an unquoted trading company resident in the UK with at least 50% of the voting shares held by employees.

s.361(3)

(e)   The payment of inheritance tax by personal representatives before a grant of representation. Interest is allowed for 12 months only.

s.364(1)

(f)   The purchase by a partner of plant or machinery used in the business. Interest is allowed only until three years from the end of the tax year in which the loan was taken out. If the plant is used partly for private purposes, then the allowable interest is proportionately reduced.

s.359(1)

(g)   The purchase by an employee of plant or machinery used by him in the performance of his duties. The interest is allowable only until three years from the end of the tax year in which the loan was taken out.

s.359(3)

(h)   The replacement of other loans qualifying under (a) to (g) above.

Interest is never allowed if it is payable under a scheme or arrangement of which the expected sole or main benefit was tax relief on the interest. Interest on an overdraft or on a credit card debt does not qualify.

2.4.5 Business interest

A taxpayer paying interest wholly and exclusively for business purposes is allowed to deduct such interest in the computation of his profit under Schedule D Case I, instead of as a charge. The interest need not fall into any of the categories outlined above, and it may be on an overdraft or a credit card debt.

Note that where interest is allowable as a Schedule D Case I deduction, the amount *payable* (on an accruals basis) is deducted. Only interest *paid* in the tax year may be set against total income as a charge.

2.4.6 Vocational training

When an individual who is aged at least 16 and is resident in the UK makes a payment for his or her own training for a National Vocational Qualification (NVQ), the payment may be made net of basic rate income tax and treated as a charge. Course fees, assessment fees and fees for receiving qualifications or being entered in an official register all qualify. However, if the trainee receives public financial assistance (such as a local authority grant or a Training for Work scheme training grant) the relief is not available. Relief is not available for someone aged under 19 who is receiving full-time education at a school. It is also not available for courses undertaken wholly or mainly for recreational purposes or as a leisure activity.

ss.32, 33 FA 1991

Relief also applies whether or not the training course is for an NVQ provided the individual is over age 30 and is paying for his own retraining for a new career on a full time course lasting between four consecutive weeks and a year.

Relief may also be obtained for payments made gross, but they will only be treated as charges if relief is specifically claimed.

2.4.7 Charges in personal tax computations

As already indicated, the gross amount of any charge is deducted from the taxpayer's income to arrive at STI.

If a charge has been paid net, the basic rate income tax deducted (24% of the gross charge) is added to tax borne to arrive at tax payable. The taxpayer has obtained tax relief because the charge has reduced his income: he cannot keep the basic rate tax as well, but must pay it to the Inland Revenue.

2.5   Allowances deducted from STI

2.5.1   Introduction

Once taxable income from all sources (assessed and taxed at source) has been aggregated and any charges on income deducted, the remainder is the taxpayer's statutory total income (STI). Two allowances, the personal allowance and the blind person's allowance, are deducted from STI. The amounts given in the following paragraphs are for 1996/97.

Other allowances are not deducted from STI, but reduce tax instead. These allowances are explained in section 2.6 below.

2.5.2   PA: personal allowance

All persons (including children) are entitled to the personal allowance of £3,765.   s.257

A person aged 65 years or over (at any time in the tax year) is entitled to an age allowance of £4,910 instead of the ordinary PA of £3,765.

Where statutory total income exceeds £15,200 the age allowance is reduced by £1 for every £2 of income over £15,200 until the allowance is reduced to £3,765.

Individuals aged 75 or over (at any time in the tax year) obtain a slightly more generous age allowance of £5,090. In all respects, the higher age allowance works in the same way as the basic age allowance, with the same income limit of £15,200.

Someone who dies in the tax year in which they would have had their 65th or 75th birthday is treated as having reached that age during the year.

2.5.3   BPA: blind person's allowance

A taxpayer who is registered with a local authority as a blind person is entitled   s.265
to an allowance of £1,250.

2.5.4   Persons resident abroad

In general, non-residents are liable to tax on income arising in the UK, but are not   s.278
entitled to allowances. However, certain people are entitled to allowances
despite being non-resident. These are:

(a)   Commonwealth citizens;

(b)   citizens of states within the European Economic Area (EEA);

(c)   individuals resident in the Isle of Man and the Channel Islands;

(d)   current or former Crown servants and their widows or widowers;

(e)   former residents who have left the country for health reasons;

(f)   missionaries.

The EEA comprises the European Union (EU) plus Norway, Liechtenstein and Iceland.

A non-resident husband who can claim the married couple's allowance (see section 2.6 below) can transfer it to his wife provided she herself is entitled to allowances.

Although s.278 relief enables a non-resident to claim allowances generally, they will not usually be able to claim blind person's allowance as non-residents cannot make the necessary registration.

A non-resident taxpayer cannot normally benefit from the tax credit on a dividend from a UK company. But, if allowances are claimed under s.278, the taxpayer may deduct tax suffered on UK dividends received in arriving at the amount he must pay by direct assessment.

One point which is sometimes examined is the fact that the benefit of ESC B13 (see 1.4.4) is not available to a non-resident who makes a s.278 claim. Hence income such as UK bank deposit interest has to be included in chargeable income.

The rules for non-residents apply both to allowances deducted from STI (the PA and the BPA) and to allowances which reduce tax (see 2.6).

2.6 Tax reducers

2.6.1 Introduction

Tax reducers are items in a personal tax computation which do not affect income, but which reduce the tax on the income. The tax reducers are as follows.

(a) Investments under the enterprise investment scheme or venture capital trust scheme

(b) Allowances: the married couple's allowance, the additional personal allowance and the widow's bereavement allowance

(c) Interest on a loan to buy the borrower's main residence

(d) Maintenance payments following the breakdown of a marriage

(e) Interest on a loan to a borrower aged at least 65 to buy an annuity if the loan must be secured on the borrower's main residence

(f) Medical insurance premiums for people aged at least 60

In case (a), the tax reduction is 20% of the investment.

In cases (b), (c) and (d), the tax reduction is 15% of the allowance or payment.

In cases (e) and (f) the tax reduction is 24% of the payment.

2.6.2 The enterprise investment scheme and venture capital trust scheme

These are schemes to allow investments in certain companies to qualify as tax reducers. Details are given in Session 6.

2.6.3 Allowances

MCA: married couple's allowance

A married man whose wife is living with him is entitled to an allowance of £1,790. In the year of marriage, this is reduced by £1,790 x 1/12 = £149.17 for each complete tax month (from the 6th of one month to the 5th of the next) which has passed before the wedding.

s.257A

The wife can unilaterally elect, by the start of the relevant tax year, to have half of the tax reduction from the MCA set against her tax instead of her husband's. Alternatively, the couple can jointly elect, by the start of the relevant tax year, to transfer half or all of the tax reduction to the wife. An election remains in force until revoked, and any revocation only applies from the following 6 April. For the year of marriage, an election may be made during the year.

s.257BA

Any MCA which turns out to be wasted (because the husband or wife has insufficient tax to reduce) may be transferred to the other spouse, by a claim made within six years after the end of the tax year (for 1995/96) or within five years of 31 January following the tax year (for 1996/97 onwards).

s.257BB

A married man, if he *or his wife is* 65 or over (at any time in the tax year), is entitled to an age allowance of £3,115 instead of the ordinary MCA of £1,790. If either spouse is 75 or over, the allowance is £3,155. Half or all of the *basic* MCA (£1,790) only may be transferred to the wife, exactly as for ordinary MCA.

s.257A (3)(4)

When statutory total income exceeds £15,200, the personal allowance given to an elderly person is reduced by half of the excess, as explained above. Once that has been reduced to £3,765, the married couple's age allowance is then reduced at the same rate, but not to below £1,790. The reduction in the married couple's age allowance always depends on the *husband's* STI.

Again, someone who dies in the tax year in which they would have had their 65th or 75th birthday is treated as having reached that age during the year.

APA: additional personal allowance

The additional personal allowance applies where the claimant has a 'qualifying child' living with him or her for the whole or part of the tax year. The child must, for at least part of the year, have his or her home with the claimant: short holiday stays are not enough. The amount of the allowance is £1,790.

s.259

The claimant must be either:

(a)   a woman who is single, or at some time in the year when the child is living with her not living with her husband; or

(b)   a man who is single, or whose wife is completely incapacitated for the *whole* of the tax year, or who does not live with his wife at all during the year.

The children in respect of whom the allowance can be claimed are:

(a)   a child aged under 16 at the beginning of the tax year;

(b)   a child aged 16 or more (with no upper age limit) at the beginning of the tax year but attending a full-time course of education at an educational establishment or a full-time course of training for at least two years with an employer.

If the child is not the taxpayer's own child, he or she must also be under 18 at the beginning of the tax year and maintained for the whole or part of that year at the expense of the taxpayer.

Only one APA per claimant is allowed, and each child can only give rise to one APA. Where more than one person is entitled to claim APA in respect of the same child, the sum of the actual income tax reductions obtained must not exceed £1,790 x 15% = £269; the APA is apportioned between the claimants to ensure that this limit is not broken. (See 2.7.5 for allowances on separation.)

s.260

Where an unmarried couple, living together as husband and wife, jointly take care of children, only one APA may be claimed, even if there are several children. The claim must be for the youngest child.

WBA: widow's bereavement allowance

This allowance (£1,790) is given to a widow (*not* to a widower) for the tax year of her husband's death and, provided she has not re-married before the beginning of the following tax year, for that following year.

s.262

If, in the year of the husband's death, part or all of the MCA has been transferred to the widow by election (and not because the husband had insufficient tax fully to benefit from the tax reduction), that MCA is transferred to the husband. However, any of that MCA which then becomes useless (because the husband does not have enough tax fully to benefit from the tax reduction) is passed back to the widow so she can benefit from it. No election is needed: these transfers of MCA are automatic.

2.6.4 Loan interest: the borrower's main residence

Interest paid on qualifying loans to buy the borrower's main residence (including a houseboat or a caravan) situated in the UK or the Republic of Ireland may qualify for tax relief but is not relieved as a charge on income. When the payment is made to a 'qualifying lender' (broadly building societies, banks and other financial institutions) it falls within the MIRAS (Mortgage Interest Relief At Source) arrangements and is paid net of 15% income tax. Thus if £100 of interest were due, the borrower would pay £85 to the lender and the Inland Revenue would pay the other £15 to the lender. Where MIRAS does not apply interest is paid gross and the 15% tax relief is given as a tax reducer.

s.353(1A)

s.369

Interest paid on an overdraft or on a credit card debt does not qualify as a tax reducer.

If the loan exceeds £30,000, only interest on the first £30,000 qualifies. The £30,000 limit applies to the aggregate of all loans, and is allocated to loans in the order in which they were taken out. Thus if someone took a loan of £25,000 from one lender and then (while it was still outstanding) a loan of £10,000 from another, the first loan and £5,000 of the second loan would qualify. There is only one £30,000 allowance per married couple.

s.355(1)

If an individual is moving residence, but instead of repaying his old loan he substitutes his new residence for his old one as security for the old loan, that loan still qualifies, but only up to the lower of £30,000 and the purchase price of the new residence.

s.357A

If the borrower ceases to use a residence as his main residence and, when he does so, intends to take steps within 12 months to dispose of it, then the loan still qualifies for 12 months (or until he abandons his intention if he does so earlier), in addition to any loan to buy a new main residence. Each loan has a £30,000 limit, so relief may be given for interest on up to £60,000. However, this extra 12 months' relief is available even if the borrower decides not to buy a new residence.

s.355(1A)

Concessions apply to two situations on marriage. Where one spouse vacates a property bought before the marriage in order to live in the home of the other spouse, a tax reduction continues to be available for interest on a loan to buy the vacated property provided that it is sold within 12 months of being vacated. Alternatively, if both spouses vacate their pre-marriage properties in order to buy a matrimonial home jointly, the bridging loan provisions apply to all three properties. Three loans, one on each property, can then qualify simultaneously (up to £30,000 for each loan).

A concession also applies where a loan is taken out to purchase property used for both residential and business purposes. The loan is treated as if it were two separate loans with the residential portion qualifying for MIRAS up to £30,000 and the business portion interest qualifying as a trading expense.

ESC A89

Residence bought by more than one borrower

The qualifying loan is also restricted to a maximum of £30,000 (the 'qualifying maximum') for any *residence* irrespective of the number of borrowers.

s.356A

The restriction to loans of up to £30,000 per residence does not apply to a loan made before 1 August 1988 (or to loans made after that date provided that before 1 August 1988 the lender agreed to make the loan and the borrower was contractually obliged to purchase the property). Note that if the existing property is sold and the pre-August 1988 loan is resecured on a new property after 15 March 1993, although interest relief is allowed to continue, the loan qualifying will be restricted to £30,000 in total.

s.356C

s.357(A)(5)

A building which is designed for permanent use as a single residence is to be treated as such, despite the fact that it may be temporarily divided into two or more separately occupied parts. This may cause practical problems, particularly with flat conversions.

s.356D

Allocation of the qualifying maximum between borrowers

Although the legislation restricts the amount of the qualifying loan, the purchasers may have nevertheless taken out more than the £30,000 of loans between them. Rules are therefore necessary to apportion the £30,000 limit. These rules vary according to which of the three following sets of circumstances apply:

s.356A

(a)   the borrowers are two or more individuals who are not married to each other;

(b)   the borrowers are a married couple; or

(c)   the borrowers are a married couple and a third party.

The general rule for unmarried homesharers is that the qualifying maximum of £30,000 is allocated equally between them. Thus, if there are three borrowers each will have a maximum qualifying loan of £10,000. But, where one of the borrowers has a smaller loan than his allocation, the remainder is reallocated to those with 'shortfalls' (ie. borrowers whose allocation is less than their loan) in proportion to their excess over the normal allocation.

Example

Alex, Bill and Cleo purchase a residence for their own occupation on 1 October 1995. Their loans for this purpose are: Alex £24,000; Cleo £16,000; and Bill £8,000. What is the qualifying loan for each of them?

Solution

	Total loan £	Normal allocation £	Excess loans £	Realloc -ation £	Qualifying amount £
Alex	24,000	10,000	14,000	1,400	11,400
Cleo	16,000	10,000	6,000	600	10,600
Bill	8,000	10,000	nil	(2,000)	8,000
	48,000	30,000			30,000

Reallocation of Bill's excess sharer's limit:

Alex: $\dfrac{£14,000}{£14,000 + 6,000} \times £2,000$ £1,400

Cleo: $\dfrac{£6,000}{£14,000 + 6,000} \times £2,000$ 600

£2,000

If the borrowers are a married couple the sharer's limit is allocated equally. However, the couple can elect to divide the interest between themselves for tax purposes in any proportion they choose even if the mortgage is in the name of one spouse only and only one spouse makes the payments.

s.356B

If the borrowers are a married couple and a third party the sharer's limit is divided three ways. Again the married couple can arrange the total relief that they are entitled to between themselves as they choose. Thus if Alex and Cleo, in the above example, were married to each other their combined qualifying amount of £22,000 (£11,400 + £10,600) could be divided between themselves in whatever proportion they choose. Their marriage would have had no effect on the reallocation of £1,400 entitlement from Bill.

Temporary absences from the main residence

A tax reduction for interest paid is generally only available when the dwelling is the borrower's main residence. However, the borrower is entitled to a tax reduction:

(a)   when he is absent for any reason, for a period of up to one year;   ESC A27

(b)   when he is absent due to the needs of his employment, for a period of up to four years. A further four years absence is permitted if he reoccupies his home for at least three months after a previous absence;   s.356(1)

(c)   when he is absent because he currently occupies 'job-related' accommodation and the interest is on a loan used to purchase a property which it is intended will become his main residence. Accommodation is job-related if:

    (i)   it is necessary for the proper performance of the duties of his employment (eg. a caretaker);   s.356(3)

    (ii)   it is provided for the better performance of the employee's duties and it is customary for employers to provide accommodation (eg. a policeman);

    (iii)   special security arrangements are in force and the employee occupies the accommodation as part of those arrangements, because there is a threat to his security.

The job-related accommodation exemption also applies to a self-employed person if he, or his spouse, is required to trade on premises provided by another person (eg. a brewery tenant).   s.356(3)(b)

Letting during periods of temporary absence

Where a taxpayer pays interest on a loan to buy his only or main residence, special rules apply where the residence is let while the owner is temporarily absent by reason of employment elsewhere.

Basically, interest paid is available as a deduction against the profits of the Schedule A business, unless an election is made for tax relief to be given by way of a tax reducer (at 15%) against any tax arising on general income.

An election must be made in writing within 12 months of the end of the tax year to which it relates. No particular form is prescribed. Issue 17 of the Tax Bulletin sets out the detailed rules on the making and withdrawal of the election.

The election mechanism also applies to loans within MIRAS. A taxpayer who wishes his loan to stay within MIRAS should make an election when dual eligibility first arises. The election can be withdrawn later, provided the time limit has not expired. If the election is not made, entitlement to MIRAS will cease.

Loans other than for purchase of the taxpayer's main residence

Interest on loans made for two other purposes qualifies as a tax reducer where the loans were taken out or agreed to before 6 April 1988. These are:

(a)   home improvement loans; and

(b)   loans made to purchase the main residence of:

     (i)   the borrower's divorced or separated spouse; or

     (ii)   the borrower's 'dependent relative' (ie. the borrower's widowed, divorced or separated mother or mother-in-law, or any other relative incapacitated by old age or infirmity).

Such loans will continue to qualify for the duration of the loan. But if the original loan is replaced with another loan (say, with another lender) relief will cease. Additionally, in the case of loans used to purchase the main residence of the borrower's divorced or separated spouse, or a dependent relative, the loan interest will continue to qualify for relief only as long as the *same* relative occupies the dwelling as their main residence. There is a £30,000 limit applicable to total borrowings in this category and earlier loans will qualify in priority to loans made at a later date.

2.6.5   Loan interest: life annuities

Interest on a loan qualifies for a tax reduction (at 24%) if: s.365

(a)   the loan is taken out by a borrower aged at least 65;

(b)   at least 90% of the loan is used to buy an annuity ending on the death of the borrower or of the last to die of several annuitants, one of whom is the borrower and all of whom are aged at least 65 when the loan is made; and

(c)   the loan is secured on land and buildings used as the only or main residence of the borrower and of all the other annuitants and owned by at least one annuitant.

Only interest on the first £30,000 of such a loan qualifies, but the borrower can obtain tax reductions in respect of interest on a £30,000 house purchase loan and a £30,000 annuity purchase loan simultaneously.

Interest on annuity purchase loans is generally (but not always) paid net of 24% tax under the MIRAS system.

2.6.6   Medical insurance premiums

A tax reduction (at 24%) is available for premiums (including insurance premium tax) paid to provide medical insurance for a UK resident individual aged at least 60, or for spouses both of whom are UK resident and at least one of whom is aged at least 60. The tax reduction is given to the payer of the premiums, who need not be the person insured, but must be UK resident. The payer must not be put in funds by another person or be entitled to any other tax deduction for the cost (for example as the insured person's employer providing a benefit to employees).   s.54 FA 1989

If a policy covers a married couple only one of whom is over 60, and that spouse dies, the tax reduction continues if the policy continues for the benefit of the other spouse.

An insurance policy may provide small cash (up to £5 per night in hospital) or other benefits in addition to cover for medical costs.

Qualifying premiums are generally (but not always) paid net of 24% tax. Thus if the premium due were £100, the person paying the premium would only pay £76 and the Inland Revenue would pay the other £24 to the insurance company.

2.6.7 Maintenance payments

All maintenance payments are made gross (without deduction of tax at source). A tax reduction is available for payments under court orders or written agreements, and for maintenance assessments under the Child Support Act 1991 (enforced by the Child Support Agency) and payments under orders made under section 106 of the Social Security Administration Act 1992. The court concerned, or the law governing the agreement, may be that of any EEA state (see 2.5.4).

s.347A

Provided that the payment is made for the benefit of the former spouse or of a child of the family and is made to the former spouse (but not directly to a child or to an agent such as a school), the payer is entitled to claim a tax reduction of 15% of the lower of:

s.347B

(a)   the payments *due* in the tax year; and

(b)   the amount of the MCA (£1,790 for 1996/97). The limit is the amount of the basic MCA, even if the payer is aged 65 or over.

The recipient is not liable to income tax on maintenance payments made, however large.

s.347A(1)(b)

Old maintenance agreements (pre 15.3.88)

If maintenance is paid under a court order or an agreement made before 15 March 1988, then the following rules apply:

(a)   Relief is available on the first £1,790 a year of payments as above (giving relief as a tax reducer, saving tax at 15% in 1996/97);

s.38(3A) FA 1988

(b)   Relief is available on payments in excess of £1,790 a year in the same way as charges on income (although the payments are not called charges), reducing taxable income. However, the charge is not allowed to exceed the maintenance payments eligible for relief in 1988/89 minus £1,790.

s.38(3) FA 1988

The recipient is taxed on the amount received under Schedule D Case III, subject to a maximum of the amount taxable in 1988/89. Thus increases in maintenance payments are exempt. In addition, provided a recipient divorced or separated spouse does not remarry, an amount up to the value of the married couple's allowance is tax free. There is no exemption for payments made directly to the children of the marriage.

s.38(4)FA 1988

s.38(5)FA 1988

The payer can make an election (which is irrevocable) to bring his maintenance payments under the rules for payments under agreements made on or after 15 March 1988. This must be made within 12 months of the end of the first tax year to which it is to apply.

s.39 FA 1988

2.6.8 Giving tax reductions

Tax reducers paid net

The following tax reducers are paid net of the appropriate tax reduction (15% or 24%).

(a)   Loan interest under MIRAS (whether the loan is used to buy the borrower's main residence or to buy a life annuity)

(b)   Medical insurance premiums (in most cases)

When a tax reducer is paid net, it should be *completely ignored* in preparing the individual's income tax computation. By paying only the net amount, the payer automatically obtains the correct tax reduction. This is so even if the payer has no income tax to reduce, or less income tax to reduce than the tax reduction: the Inland Revenue still subsidises the interest or premium.

Other tax reducers

Investments under the enterprise investment scheme or venture capital trust scheme, allowances, interest outside MIRAS, a few medical insurance premiums and all maintenance payments must be taken into account in preparing an individual's income tax computation. The tax reduction must be worked out, and it can then only be given if the individual has enough tax to reduce. If, for example, the tax is £230 and the reduction is £268, the tax is only reduced to nil. The individual *cannot* claim a repayment of £(268 - 230) = £38.

ss.256(2), 289(2), 347B(5A), 3(1F); s.54(3A) FA 1989

The tax which can be reduced is the tax at 20%, 24% and 40% on taxable income. It does not include tax retained on charges paid net.

ss.256(3), 89A(5), 47B(5B), 353(1H); s.54(3C) FA 1989

An individual may be entitled to several different tax reducers. In such cases they must be applied in a set order, and we must stop when the tax is reduced to nil.

The order is as follows.

(a)   Investments under the venture capital trust and enterprise investment schemes

s.289A(5)

(b)   Medical insurance premiums

s.54(3C) FA 1989

(c)   Maintenance payments and interest paid (either may be dealt with before the other)

ss.347B(5B), 353(1H)

(d)   The additional personal allowance

s.256(3)

(e)   The widow's bereavement allowance

s.256(3)

(f)   The married couple's allowance

s.256(3)

Example

Peter, a married man aged 42, pays maintenance of £3,000 a year to a former wife (maintenance agreement made in 1990). His current wife has no income. Show his tax position for 1996/97 if his income consists of:

(a)   trading profits of £21,000 and building society interest of £1,600 net;

(b)   trading profits of £2,000 and building society interest of £1,600 net.

Solution

	(a) £	(b) £
Schedule D Case I	21,000	2,000
Building society interest £1,600 x 100/80	2,000	2,000
STI	23,000	4,000
Less personal allowance	(3,765)	(3,765)
	£19,235	£235
Income tax		
£3,900/£235 x 20%	780	47
£15,335 x 24%	3,680	
	4,460	47
Tax reducers		
Maintenance payment £1,790 (limit) x 15%	(269)	(47)
	4,191	nil
Married couple's allowance £1,790 x 15%	(269)	
Tax borne and tax liability	3,922	nil
Tax suffered on building society interest £2,000 x 20%	(400)	(400)
Tax payable/(repayable)	£3,522	£(400)

Tax reducers cannot lead to repayments of tax, so in (b) the MCA is wasted. However, tax suffered on income can be repaid. If Peter's wife had had income of her own, the surplus MCA could have been transferred to her.

2.7 Husbands, wives and children

2.7.1 Introduction

Husband and wife are taxed as two separate people. Each makes their own tax returns and claims, and has their own tax computation. The general position on allowances (PA, MCA, APA, WBA and transfer of surplus MCA) has been set out in sections 2.5 and 2.6 above.

Tax law only recognises legal marriages, not "common law" marriages.

Rignell v Andrews (1990)

2.7.2 Joint property

Where a husband and wife jointly own income generating property, it is assumed that they are entitled to equal shares of the income.

s.282A

The presumption of equal shares does not apply:

(a) to earned income eg. under Schedule E;

(b) to partnership income under Schedule D Case I or II;

(c) where the couple have separated;

(d) where other legislation provides for income to be taxed in a particular way (eg. where the income arises from a settlement);

(e) where the property is beneficially owned by both spouses but is held in the name of only one spouse. This results in a trust and income will be split for tax purposes on the basis of each spouse's entitlement; and

(f) where neither spouse is beneficially entitled to income arising from the property (eg. where they hold the property as trustees and neither spouse is a beneficiary).

If a new asset is acquired in joint names and special commencement rules apply, the commencement rules must apply to each spouse's half share of the income.

If an asset which was held by only one spouse is transferred into joint names and special cessation rules apply, the cessation rules apply to the half share disposed of by the spouse originally holding the asset. The commencement rules then apply to income arising on the half share for the spouse who has become a joint holder.

The equal shares rule only applies to income arising after the joint ownership commences. Where an asset is transferred into joint names having been held by one spouse only, the spouse acquiring a share is taxed on half the income arising from that date, not on half the whole income arising from that source in the current or previous year.

The equal shares rule ceases to apply where either the husband or wife dies. For income assessed on a preceding year basis the normal cessation rules apply in theory to the share of the spouse who dies. However, under ESC A7 income assessed under Schedule D Cases III, IV or V in such circumstances will continue to be assessed on a preceding year basis provided the surviving spouse inherits the source in its entirety. It is open to the personal representative or the surviving spouse to request the correct cessation/commencement treatment instead. This concession is not required for income taxed on the current year basis.

If the couple separate the equal shares rule is discontinued. If an asset held in joint names is assessed on a preceding year basis and remains in joint names after separation the cessation/commencement rules will not apply if each spouse actually has an equal share in the asset and its income.

The couple can make a joint declaration of their actual beneficial interests in an asset held in joint names if their actual entitlements to the asset and its income are unequal. This will result in the income being assessed on each spouse according to their actual share.

s.282B

There is no requirement that the couple make such a declaration where their interests are unequal. In fact a declaration need only include those assets which the couple choose to include. If a declaration is made for an asset it must show the actual split of the beneficial interests. A declaration can only be made for an asset if the split of interests in the asset is the same as the split of interests in the income.

Example

David owns an office which he lets. He transfers a beneficial interest in 5% of the asset to his wife, Joan, but transfers a beneficial interest in 95% of the income to her.

You are required to state whether a joint declaration of beneficial interest can be made.

Solution

They cannot make a joint declaration of actual interests in the property, as their interests in the asset differ from their interests in the income. They will instead be treated as though the income arose equally between them.

In fact income can be shifted for tax purposes between spouses by the simple expedient of allowing the Revenue to apply the equal shares rule when only a small beneficial interest is transferred.

A declaration is invalid if it is not submitted within 60 days of the date it is made. Income will be split on the basis of the declaration from the date of the declaration. A declaration in respect of an asset cannot be withdrawn and remains in force until either the marriage comes to an end or the beneficial interests change.

If a declaration is invalidated by a change of beneficial interests the equal shares rule applies until a further declaration is made. Obviously if an asset covered by a declaration ceases to be held in joint names, the spouse beneficially entitled to the income from the asset will be assessed on it from the date of the change.

s.660A (6)

If one spouse's marginal rate of tax (the rate on the highest part of his or her income) is higher than the other spouse's marginal rate, it is sensible to transfer income-yielding assets to the spouse with the lower rate. Income might then, for example, be taxed at 20 or 24% instead of at 40%. However, an outright gift of the property (with no strings attached) is required.

2.7.3 The year of marriage

s.257A(6)

The husband receives part of the married couple's allowance (MCA). He receives the full amount less 1/12 of £1,790 for each complete tax month during which the couple were *unmarried*. A tax month runs from the 6th of one month to the 5th of the next month. The amounts which may be transferred by election are half or all of this reduced MCA.

If a married couple separate in one tax year but are reconciled in a later year, the husband receives the full MCA (ie. not reduced as for the date of marriage) in the year of reconciliation, provided they had not divorced in the meantime.

Where the age related MCA (see para 2.6.3) is due in the year of marriage, the full allowance is first reduced, if necessary, to take account of the claimant's income in excess of the income limit and the net MCA is then reduced by 1/12 for each tax month elapsing before the date of the marriage.

A woman cannot claim an APA for the year of marriage unless the child in respect of whom APA is claimed was resident with her prior to the marriage.

If a man marries during a year of assessment, and would otherwise have been entitled to claim an APA, he may elect to disregard the marriage and claim an APA rather than the MCA. This will generally be beneficial, unless he marries before 6th May in the year of assessment. However, a husband who has no income, or only a small income, and whose wife is liable to tax may benefit from claiming a reduced MCA rather than an APA as the surplus MCA can be transferred to his wife. (The surplus APA cannot be transferred.)

2.7.4   The year of death

If a wife dies during a tax year her widower receives the personal allowance (PA) and a full MCA for that year. The wife will have a full PA to cover income to the date of death.

When a husband dies, his tax affairs up to the date of his death are dealt with on the basis of his receiving the full PA and MCA. Any election relating to the MCA thus becomes void in the year of death. The widow obtains her PA for the year, plus a full APA if she has the care of children and, in the tax year of her bereavement, WBA. The WBA is also given in the following tax year if she has not remarried before the beginning of that year.

2.7.5   Divorce and separation

Divorce is usually preceded by separation. Where a couple become separated under a court order or separation deed, or in circumstances such that the separation is likely to be permanent, they are then taxed as single people from the date of separation.

In the tax year in which the separation takes place, however, the husband receives the PA plus a full MCA. However, any election as to the MCA remains valid.

The ex wife and/or the husband will be able to obtain the APA (partly, or in full) for the year of separation if she/he has custody of one or more children. The APA will then be available in full to either/both in subsequent years, as appropriate.

The tax reduction for the APA is always given before that for the MCA. There is however a special rule when an individual claims both the APA and all or half of the MCA for the year when spouses separate. The tax reduction for the APA is reduced by £1,790 x 15% = £269, or by £269/2 = £135 if only half of the MCA is being claimed. This applies even if the individual's tax is so low that a full tax reduction of £269 or £135 for the MCA would not be obtained. Thus the maximum ACA + MCA that can be claimed by an individual in the year of separation will be £1,790 @ 15% = £269. s.261(a)

2.7.6   Minor children

There is legislation to prevent the parent of a minor child transferring income to the child in order to use the child's personal allowance and lower and basic rate tax bands. Income which is directly transferred by the parent, or is derived from capital so transferred, remains income of the parent for tax purposes. The legislation applies only to parents, however, and tax saving is therefore possible by other relatives making the transfer. Even where a parent is involved, the child's income is not treated as the parent's if it does not exceed £100 a year. s.660B

This legislation is concerned with gifts from a parent to a child. It may therefore be possible to use the child's personal allowance and lower and basic rate bands if the child is instead employed in the parent's trade. But a deduction for wages (in working out the business's taxable profits) will be permitted only if the wages are reasonable in relation to the work done. Copeman v Wm
Flood & Sons Ltd
(1940)
Dollar v Lyon
(1981)

2.8   Exempt income

To conclude this chapter here is an abbreviated list of the main types of income exempted from income tax:

(a)	scholarship income (exempt only in the hands of the scholar: taxable on parent if paid by parent's employer);	s.331
(b)	winnings from betting and gaming;	
(c)	gifts;	
(d)	many social security benefits, in particular child benefit, although unemployment benefit and the state pension are taxable;	s.617
(e)	interest or terminal bonus on UK National Savings certificates and prizes on premium bonds;	s.46
(f)	the first £30,000 of certain compensation payments received on termination of employment;	s.188
(g)	interest on damages for personal injuries;	s.329
(h)	insurance benefits paid in the event of accident, sickness, disability or unemployment (including mortgage payment protection insurance benefit) except where the premiums received tax relief;	ss.580A & 580B
(i)	the first £70 interest on National Savings Bank *ordinary* accounts;	s.325
(j)	a terminal bonus paid under a 'contractual savings scheme';	s.326
(k)	interest on certain government stocks held by persons not ordinarily resident in the UK;	s.47
(l)	interest on tax exempt special savings accounts (TESSAs);	s.326A
(m)	dividends and interest received in a personal equity plan (PEP);	s.333
(n)	up to £3,250 gross letting income from letting furnished accommodation in the landlord's own main residence;	Sch 10 F(No.2)A 1992
(o)	dividends on ordinary shares in a Venture Capital Trust (up to the permitted maximum £100,000 investment per year).	
(p)	annuity or periodical payments received as damages for personal injury;	ss.329 AA, 329 AB

Note that the exemptions in (b) and (c) above do not derive from statute, but from the general principle that income is taxable only if, amongst other things, it arises from a *source*. Neither gambling winnings nor gifts have a source and hence they are non-taxable.

QUESTIONS

1. Define "statutory total income".

2. Give the Schedule (and Case, if appropriate) under which the following types of income will be assessed:
    (a) rental income from letting property in Glasgow;
    (b) rental income from letting property in Marbella;
    (c) the profits of a firm of accountants;
    (d) the salary of an individual employed by a firm of accountants.

3. On 31 December 1996, an individual receives a UK dividend of £832. Compute the amount of taxable income.

4. Jack (aged 62) is married to Elsie (aged 67). To what allowances is Jack entitled in 1996/97, assuming his STI amounts to £15,800 and his wife's STI is £5,400?

5. Oberon and Titania married on 24 September 1996. What allowances is Oberon entitled to in 1996/97 ignoring the possibility of Titania making an election?

6. If Oberon (question 5 above) had in his care his daughter (aged 9) from a previous marriage, how would this affect your answer?

7. In which year(s) of assessment is a widow entitled to widow's bereavement allowance?

8. Interest on a loan to purchase the taxpayer's only or main residence qualifies as a tax reducer only if, amongst other things, the property is situated in the UK. TRUE/FALSE?

9. Bill and Ben purchase a property jointly on 1 December 1996. Bill takes out a loan of £12,000, whereas Ben takes out a loan of £20,000. Interest paid on how much of each loan is a tax reducer, assuming the property constitutes the main residence of each borrower?

10. Peter pays Rita £250 per month under a separation agreement which they drew up, after they decided to separate, on 1 August 1996. Payments are made on the last day of each month.
    (a) Should Peter make the payments net of income tax or gross?
    (b) What tax reductions is Peter entitled to in 1996/97?
    Assume that neither party has remarried.

11.   James has an investment property on which rents received suffer income tax at 40%. His wife Jill has insufficient income to utilise her personal allowance so he wishes to transfer the income to her for tax purposes. Which of the following statements are correct?

(a)   He can transfer the property into her name, on condition she hands over the income to him, and the income will be taxed on her.

(b)   He can transfer the property into her name, let her use the income as she chooses but require her to leave the property to him in her will and the income will be taxed on her.

(c)   He can transfer the property into joint names with his wife, retain a 95% beneficial interest, and thereby transfer half the income to her.

(d)   Under (c) he could declare that 95% of the income was hers.

SOLUTIONS

1. STI: total income (from all sources) less charges on income (2.1).

2. (a) Schedule A
    (b) Schedule D Case V
    (c) Schedule D Case II
    (d) Schedule E.
    (2.2.2)

3. £1,040 ie. £832 x 100/80 (2.2.3).

4. Personal allowance of £3,765 and married couple's allowance of £3,115 - [£(15,800 - 15,200) x 0.5] = £2,815 (because one spouse is aged 65 or over) (2.5.2 and 2.6.3).

5. Personal allowance: £3,765

    MCA: (7/12 x £1,790) = £1,044. (2.5.2 and 2.6.3).

6. Oberon should forgo his right to the scaled-down married couple's allowance in 1996/97, and claim instead the APA of £1,790 (2.7.3).

7. (a) In the year of assessment in which her husband dies; and
    (b) the following year, provided she has not remarried before the start of that year.

    (2.6.3)

8. FALSE - the property could, alternatively, be situated in the Republic of Ireland (2.6.4).

9. In principle, the limit of £30,000 is split equally between them, ie. £15,000 each. But Bill's "excess allocation" of £3,000 (£15,000 - 12,000) is transferred to Ben. Hence Bill is entitled to relief on interest on a loan of £12,000 (ie. all the interest he pays is a tax reducer). Ben is entitled to relief on interest on £18,000 (£15,000 + 3,000) out of his loan of £20,000. (2.6.4).

10. (a) Gross
    (b) Lower of
        (i)   payments due: £250 x 8 = £2,000; and
        (ii) £1,790.
            ie. £1,790 (tax reduction £1,790 x 15% = £269) (2.6.7)

11. (a) and (b) are FALSE as the property must be transferred without 'strings attached'.

(c) is correct as income on jointly held property is deemed to be shared equally.

(d) is false. A joint declaration can be made to overturn the 50:50 split assumption but it can only change the split to the actual proportions of beneficial ownership. (2.7.2)

SESSION 3

DEALING WITH THE INLAND REVENUE

The purpose of this session is to describe the administrative system used by the Revenue relating to the assessing and collecting of tax covering:

- the self assessment regime applying for 1996/97 onwards
- the old regime applying up to 1995/96

References: TMA 1970 unless otherwise stated.

3.1   Introduction to tax management

This session is devoted to contact with the Inland Revenue to settle a taxpayer's income tax and CGT liability, a subject which features regularly in examinations.

Substantial changes have been made to the administrative system and come into effect for 1996/97 and subsequent years. We will deal firstly with the new rules and then with the old rules.

In order to avoid confusion between the two, examples under old provisions are for the 1994/95 year of assessment, and those under the new are for the 1997/98 year of assessment.

The self-assessment rules are covered first in sections 3.2 to 3.6.

The old rules are then explained in sections 3.7 to 3.12.

THE SELF-ASSESSMENT RULES

3.2 Introduction to self-assessment

Essentially, the new rules for disclosing sources of income and gains to the Revenue and subsequently accounting for any tax thereon, can be broken down as follows:

(a) Notifying chargeability to tax

(b) Submitting a tax return

(c) Paying the tax

Although the first self assessment return will not be issued until April 1997 - the '1996/97 return' - the first payment under the new system is due on 31 January 1997. The Revenue will advise taxpayers of any amount due on that date based on the previous year's known income.

3.3 Notifying chargeability to tax

For 1995/96 and subsequent years of assessment, individuals who are chargeable to income tax or capital gains tax for any year of assessment and who have not received a tax return will be required to give notice of chargeability to an officer of the Board within six months from the end of the tax year ie. by 5 October 1998 for 1997/98.

FA1994 Sch. 19
para. 1
s.7(1) & (2)

A person who has no chargeable gains and who is not liable to higher rate tax does not have to give notice of chargeability if all his income:

s.7 (3) - (7)

(a) Has been subject to PAYE

(b) Is not liable to tax under a self-assessment

(c) Has had income tax deducted at source; or

(d) Is chargeable to tax under Schedule F (eg. a UK dividend)

The maximum (mitigable) penalty where notice of chargeability is not given is 100% of the tax assessed which is not paid on or before the 31 January next following the tax year; ie. for 1997/98, by 31 January 1999.

s.7(8)

Note that the self-assessment version of s.7 was brought in a year in advance of the self-assessment regime ie. 1995/96 in advance of 1996/97.

3.4   Tax returns

3.4.1   Introduction

Self-assessment returns must be submitted by 31 January after the end of the tax year, or if later, three months after the issue of a tax return.   s.9(1)

The return contains a self-assessment section in which the taxpayer will normally be expected to calculate his income tax and capital gains tax liability for the year of assessment to which the return relates.

However, a self-assessment is voluntary, at least to the extent that there is no obligation for the taxpayer to self-assess if the completed return is delivered to an officer of the Board by no later than:

- 30 September following the tax year to which it relates; or

- if later, within 2 months after the notice to make the return was issued.   s.9(2)

Where a tax return is delivered to the Revenue within the above time limits an officer must make an assessment on the taxpayer's behalf on the basis of the information contained in the return, and must send a copy of the assessment to the taxpayer. Such assessments - even though raised by the Revenue - are to be treated as self-assessments.   s.9(3)

Where a tax return is delivered to the Revenue after the deadline for opting out of self-assessment (eg. for 1997/98, normally 30 September 1998) and the taxpayer has not completed the self-assessment section of the return, it would appear that the Revenue will be able to reject the return as incomplete and force the taxpayer to self-assess. In practice - particularly where the return is delivered shortly after 30 September - it is thought the Revenue will accept many such returns and that an officer will then raise an assessment based on the information contained in the return. Any such assessment will be treated as a self-assessment.   s.9(3)

Within 9 months of receiving a tax return, the Revenue have the power to amend a taxpayer's self-assessment to correct any obvious errors or mistakes in the return; whether errors of principle, arithmetical mistakes or otherwise.   s.9(4)(a)

Within 12 months of the due filing date (*not* the actual filing date), the taxpayer has the right to give notice to an officer to amend his tax return and self-assessment. Such amendments by taxpayers are not confined to the correction of obvious errors.   s.9(4)(b)

The Revenue have the power to enquire into the completeness and accuracy of any return under self-assessment provided they issue a written notice of enquiry within 12 months of the 31 January filing date. If a return is filed or amended after the 31 January filing date the Revenue can issue the notice of enquiry within 12 months of the end of the calendar quarter in which the return was filed/amended.   s.9A

3.4.2   Penalties for late delivery

In outline, the maximum penalties for late delivery of a tax return will be:

Return delivered	Penalty
Within 6 months following the due filing date	£100
More than 6 months but not more than 12 months following the due filing date	£200
More than 12 months following the due filing date	£200 + 100% of the tax liability shown in the return

In addition, the General or Special Commissioners can direct that a maximum penalty of £60 per day be imposed where failure to deliver a tax return continues after notice of the direction has been given to the taxpayer. s.93

The fixed penalties of £100/£200 can be set aside by the Commissioners if they are satisfied that the taxpayer had a reasonable excuse for not delivering the return. The tax geared penalty is mitigable by the Revenue or the Commissioners.

3.4.3 Partnership Returns and Statements

For 1996/97 onwards partnerships will be required to file separate returns which will have to include "a partnership statement" (see below). The partnership return will normally be made by the senior partner (or whoever else may be nominated by the partnership), but the Revenue have power to require any, all, or some of the partners to submit the return. s.12AA

Every partnership return will have to include a declaration of the name, residence and tax reference of each partner, as well as the usual declaration that the return is correct and complete to the best of the signatory's knowledge. s. 12AA(6)

The normal due filing date for a partnership tax return is 31 January following the tax year to which the return relates or, if later, 3 months after the notice to make the return was issued by the Revenue. s.12AA(4)

The maximum penalties for late delivery of a partnership tax return will be as shown in para 3.4.2 above, save that there is no tax-geared penalty if the return is more than 12 months late. It should be noted that such penalties apply separately to each partner. s.93A

Each partnership tax return will be incomplete unless it includes a partnership statement showing s.12AB

(a) the amount of the adjusted partnership income or loss from each source, and any partnership charges on income, for each period of account ending in the year of assessment to which the partnership return relates; and

(b) the allocation of such income, losses and charges between each individual partner. s.12AB(1)

3.4.4 Claims for reliefs

For 1996/97 onwards the basic rule is that all claims and elections which can be made in a tax return must be made in this manner if a return has been issued by the Revenue.

Although a claim may need the approval of the Revenue, provided the necessary conditions for a relief exist, a taxpayer may apply a relief in his self-assessment without prior approval by the Revenue.

Claims for any relief, allowance or repayment of tax must be quantified at the time the claim is made. However, this does not apply to claims to carry back loss relief to an earlier year or to claims that can be dealt with through the PAYE system (eg. by amending a code number).

Where relief for a loss, etc. is carried back to an earlier year of assessment:

(a) the claim for relief is treated as made in relation to the year in which the loss was actually incurred;

(b) the amount of any tax repayment due is calculated in terms of tax of the earlier years to which the loss is being carried back; and s.42

(c) any tax repayment, etc. is treated as relating to the later year in which the loss was actually incurred. s.42(1)-(3)

Thus, a trading loss carried back can only give rise to a repayment supplement (ie. interest on overpaid tax) from the 1 February next following the end of the tax year in which the loss was actually incurred.

s.42(3A) & (3B)

Claims and elections which cannot be made in a tax return are governed by separate provisions which are similar to the rules governing the treatment of returns under self-assessment.

Sch. 1A

For 1996/97 onwards capital losses will only be allowable for CGT purposes if notified to an officer of the Board and such notification will be treated as a claim for relief for the year in which the loss accrues. Therefore, notification of such losses will have to be made within 5 years from 31 January following the year of assessment in which they accrued.

TCGA 1992
s.16(2A)

Losses for 1996/97 and subsequent years (notified as above) are to be treated as relieved against chargeable gains in priority to losses that accrued prior to 1996/97.

s.43

The references to specific claims should be easier to understand when you revise this paragraph having studied the rest of the syllabus.

3.4.5 Keeping of Records

For 1996/97 onwards taxpayers have a legal requirement to keep and retain all records to enable them to make and deliver a correct tax return.

s.12B

Records must be retained until enquiries by the Revenue into the return can no longer be commenced, or until such enquiries have been completed, whichever is the later. Where a person receives a tax return after the normal record keeping period has expired, he must keep all records in his possession at that time until no enquiries can be raised in respect of the return or until such enquiries have been completed.

The maximum (mitigable) penalty for each failure to keep and retain records is £3,000 per tax year.

s.12B(5)

3.4.6 Discovery assessments

An assessment may be issued by the Revenue to make good any tax lost if an officer of the Board or the Board *discovers* that income which should have been assessed has not been assessed or that too little has been assessed. The word *discover* has been given a very wide meaning.

s.29(3)

An inspector settled appeals against assessments following submission of the accounts. However, a different inspector later took a different view about an item included in the accounts and issued an additional assessment. It was held that although there had been a discovery, the inspector was not entitled to raise the additional assessment since the point in dispute had been agreed under s.54 TMA 1970, when the appeal was determined.

Cenlon Finance
Co Ltd v
Ellwood (1962)

However, an inspector was prevented from 'discovering' and raising an additional assessment where sufficient information was disclosed in agreeing the original assessment to enable an "ordinarily competent" inspector to decide what the liability should be. The fact that he makes some error, eg. incorrect admission of a loss relief claim, did not enable the same or another inspector to issue a further assessment once the error comes to light.

Scorer v Olin
Energy Systems
Ltd. (1985)

A Statement of Practice sets out the Revenue's view of the principle established in the *Cenlon Finance Co Ltd v Ellwood* and *Scorer v Olin Energy Systems Ltd.* Discovery assessments were not made if the facts were fully disclosed and the inspector's original decision was tenable given the law and practice at the time.

SP8/91

If a return has been made by the taxpayer and full disclosure has been made, generally a discovery assessment cannot be made. A discovery assessment can only be made either if there has been a loss of tax as a result of fraudulent or negligent conduct by the taxpayer or his agent or the officer could not realistically have been expected to have identified the circumstances giving rise to the loss of tax on the evidence then made available to him. Time limits for discovery assessments are five years from 31 January following the tax year where there has simply been incomplete disclosure and twenty years from 31 January following the tax year where there has been fraudulent or negligent conduct.

3.4.7 The Inland Revenue Adjudicator

The Inland Revenue Adjudicator is independent of the Inland Revenue. The adjudicator considers complaints about the way in which the Inland Revenue have handled a taxpayer's affairs, for example complaints about delays or the Inland Revenue's exercise of its discretion, but does not consider complaints where there are alternative channels of appeal; thus appeals against assessments, for example, go to the Commissioners. The Inland Revenue will accept the adjudicator's decision unless there are exceptional circumstances.

3.4.8 The Taxpayer's Charter

The Taxpayer's Charter lays down standards for the Inland Revenue in its dealings with taxpayers. Codes of practice give more detailed guidance on particular aspects of the Inland Revenue's work.

3.4.9 Disputes with the Revenue

If the Revenue enquire into self-assessments or make discovery assessments and there is then a dispute between the Revenue and the taxpayer, an appeal can be made by either side to the General or Special commissioners (see 1.3.2).

3.5   Payment of Tax

3.5.1   Main rules

Payments on account of income tax will be due on 31 January in the tax year and 31 July immediately following the tax year.

The amounts of these interim payments will normally be equal to one-half of the total income tax liability (less any tax deducted at source) for the previous year.

The balance of the income tax liability and the whole of the CGT liability will be due on 31 January following the tax year. The only exception to this is where the taxpayer has given notice of liability to tax within six months of the end of the tax year, but the tax return is issued after 31 October following the tax year. In this case, the due date for the final liability is three months from the issue of the tax return.

Payments on account will not be required where substantially all of the taxpayer's income is subject to deduction of tax at source, or where the amount is below an as yet to be specified de minimis limit.

If the taxpayer believes that his liability for the current year is lower than that of the previous year, he is permitted to reduce the payment. A claim must be submitted specifying the reason. The Revenue may impose a penalty of up to 100% of the excess of 50% of the previous year's tax over the tax paid, if it can show fraud or negligence.

If the current year's liability is likely to be higher than that of the preceding year, there is no requirement to increase the interim payments.

Interim payments of CGT are not required. The whole of the tax is payable on 31 January after the end of the tax year.

If a return is amended, any additional tax is payable within 30 days of the amendment if this is later than 31 January.

3.5.2   Transitional rules for 1996/97

Interim payments due for 1996/97 are determined by transitional rules.

These rules provide that the payment on account on 31 January 1997 does not exceed payments of tax made for Schedule A and Schedule D Cases I - VI for 1995/96 on 1 January 1996. The payment due on 31 July 1997 will not exceed the second 1995/96 Schedule D Case I instalment paid on 1 July 1996.

Accordingly, no payment on account has to be made (in 1996/97 only!) for higher rate tax due on taxed investment income, and for additional tax due, for example, on benefits-in-kind.

Example

Olivia has various sources of income that give rise to a 1995/96 tax liability as follows:

Sch D Case II	£12,000
Sch D Case III (gross)	£1,000
Sch A	£1,000
Dividends	£4,500
Bank interest (net)	£900

What are her required payments on account for 1996/97?

Solution

	31.1.97 £	31.7.97 £	Total £
Case II	6,000	6,000	12,000
Case III	1,000	-	1,000
Sch A	1,000	-	1,000
	£8,000	£6,000	£14,000

No payments on account required for taxed income (eg. dividends, bank interest).

3.6   Surcharges and interest on late payments

3.6.1   Surcharges on unpaid tax

The following surcharges will normally be imposed in respect of the final balance of income tax and capital gains tax paid late:

- tax paid within 28 days of due date:	0%	s.59C(1) - (3)
- tax paid more than 28 days but not more than 6 months after the due date:	5%	
- tax paid more than 6 months after the due date:	10%	

The surcharge rules do not apply to late payments on account of income tax.   s.59C(1)

The surcharge provisions have been extended to income tax and capital gains tax   FA 1995 s.109(2)
assessments for 1995/96 and earlier years which are made on or after 6 April 1998.
Therefore, any tax charged by such an assessment which is not paid within 28
days of the due date will attract a 5% surcharge (10% if paid more than 6 months
after the due date).

3.6.2   Interest on overdue tax

Under self asssessment, the basic rule is that interest is chargeable on the late   s.86
payment of both payments on account of income tax (under s.59A) and payments of
income tax and capital gains tax (under s.59B). In both cases it is assumed that
the previous interpretation of the period for which interest will run still applies
ie. interest will run from the due and payable date until the day before the actual
date of payment.

Therefore, in respect of (i) tax payable following an amendment to a self-
assessment made after the 31 January next following the year of assessment, (ii)
tax payable in a discovery assessment, and (iii) tax postponed under an appeal
which becomes payable, interest will usually be charged from the 31 January next
following the year of assessment until the day before the date of payment.

There are complicated rules governing the calculation of interest where a   s.86(4) - (6)
taxpayer makes a claim to reduce his payments on account and there is still a
final payment to be made. The basic rule is that interest is charged on the
payments on account as if each of those payments had been the lower of:

-     the reduced amount, plus 50% of the final income tax liability;

-     the amount which would have been payable had no claim for reduction
        been made.

Where interest has been charged on late interim payments of income tax and the   s.86(7) - (9)
final settlement on the 31 January next following the year of assessment produces
an income tax repayment, all or part of the original interest payable is to be
remitted.

Interest is also chargeable on the surcharge if paid more than 30 days after it is   s.59C(6)
imposed.

The self-assessment interest provisions also apply to income tax and capital gains   FA 1995
tax assessments for 1995/96 and earlier years which are made on or after 6 April   s.110(2))
1998.

Example

Fergus pays a relevant amount of income tax of £15,000 for 1996/97. In 1997/98, he has an overall income tax liability of £24,000 of which £8,000 is deducted at source, and also has capital gains tax to pay of £3,000.

You are required to state when Fergus should make payments to avoid any interest or surcharge on late paid tax.

Solution

1997/98:

31.1.98	s.59A -	50% x relevant amount for 1996/97 ie. 50% x £15,000		£7,500
31.7.98	s.59A -	as for first payment on account		£7,500
31.1.99	s.59B -	£24,000 - 8,000 - 15,000	=	1,000
		+ capital gains tax		3,000
				£4,000

Example

Following on from the example above, Fergus was issued with a tax return for 1997/98 on 1 December 1998, having submitted a notification of chargeability on 1 September 1998. He completed the return and submitted it, together with the appropriate payment under s.59B TMA 1970, on 31 March 1999. The payments due under s.59A had been made on time for 1997/98.

You are required to describe the action that could be taken by the Revenue.

Solution

1. Notification of chargeability was made on time - no penalty.

2. Tax return due for submission on, or before, 1 March 1999 (3 months after issue)

    -   penalty for late submission within 6 months of due date is £100 unless Fergus has 'reasonable excuse'.

3. Payment due under s.59B made more than 28 days after it was due

    -   surcharge of 5% x £4,000 = £200 under s.59C would be due.

4. Interest on late paid tax under s.86 TMA 1970 will be due on the s.59B payment, and also on the surcharge if not paid within 30 days of being levied by the Revenue.

Example

Simon pays a relevant amount of income tax of £10,000 in 1996/7. He pays £5,000 on account of tax for 1997/98 on each of 13 February 1998 and 21 August 1998. His income tax liability for 1997/98 is £12,000. He pays the additional amount due on 19 February 1999.

You are required to show the interest due on late payments. Assume a rate of interest of 10% and work to the nearest day and penny.

Solution

1st payment due 31.1.98 paid 13.2.98

Interest due $\dfrac{13}{365}$ x 10% x £5,000 =   £17.81

2nd payment due 31.7.98 paid 21.8.98

Interest due $\dfrac{21}{365}$ x 10% x £5,000 =   £28.77

Final payment due 31.1.99 paid 19.2.99

Interest due $\dfrac{19}{365}$ x 10% x £(12,000 - 10,000) = £10.41

3.6.3 Interest on repayments of tax

Interest runs on balancing repayments from the due date for payment (or, if later, the actual date of payment) to the date the repayment is made.

THE OLD RULES

3.7 Introduction to the old rules

The old 'pre-self-assessment' rules were time honoured but rather cumbersome and too complicated for a tax management system that was (at least theoretically) accessible to the tax paying public without recourse to professional assistance.

The old rules are still examinable as they apply for 1995/96. They may be viewed as having four aspects, as follows:

(a)   Making returns of income to the inspector

(b)   Dealing with assessments

(c)   Payment dates; and

(d)   Interest on tax (late payment and repayment supplements)

Each of these is dealt with in turn.

As a starting point, you must be aware of the organisation of the Inland Revenue, which was outlined in session 1.3.

3.8 Returns and penalties

3.8.1 Making a return

We referred to the Inspector's work in Session 1 as consisting partly of examining completed '*returns*'. At the beginning of each fiscal year the Inland Revenue sends tax return forms to taxpayers. The taxpayer should complete his or her return and submit it to the inspector within 30 days of receiving it. The forms are detailed documents and are concerned to establish the two main features of a taxpayer's circumstances, namely the amount of his or her income (and capital gains) and the reliefs claimed.

s.8

A return must be signed by the taxpayer. Another person (legally empowered) may only sign if the taxpayer is physically or mentally incapable of signing.

Full accounts of businesses are normally required. But where the taxpayer has income from a trade or from letting property, and the annual turnover or gross rent is less than £15,000, the return may include '3-line accounts', showing turnover, total expenses and profit. The Inspector may require full accounts in particular cases.

Details of an individual's disposals chargeable to capital gains tax are included as part of his normal tax return, except that a simplified return may be made if the conditions to do so are satisfied. Detailed computations are not needed if chargeable gains do not exceed the amount of the annual exemption and the aggregate consideration received does not exceed an amount equal to twice the annual exemption.

Details still need to be submitted if there are any losses to carry forward.

3.8.2 Penalties

A *1995/96* tax return form would have been sent to taxpayers in *April 1995* and would have required the taxpayer to enter on it all details of income from all sources and capital gains for the year to *5 April 1995* and to claim allowances and reliefs for the year to *5 April 1996*. Any person, when notice is given to him by the inspector or other officer of the Board, was required to make a return of his income (and gains) from every source. In practice, the 30 day time limit for submitting the form to the inspector was not strictly adhered to, but a penalty for late submission could be imposed. The maximum penalty was £300, plus £60 per day after the hearing of proceedings. If a return was not submitted by the end of the year of assessment following the year in which it was issued, there was an additional penalty of up to the tax due on the income that should have been declared on the overdue return. This was in addition to the tax itself. The Revenue had powers to mitigate these penalties.

s.93

It would be impossible for the Inland Revenue to have issued return forms to every potential taxpayer and indeed this did not happen every year. But where no return form was issued and an individual was chargeable to income tax (or capital gains tax), he had to notify the inspector that he was so chargeable within one year after the end of the year of assessment for which he was chargeable.

ss.7 & 12

The one year time limit applied up to 1994/95 but was reduced to six months for 1995/96 onwards. Thus a source acquired in 1995/96 had to be notified by 6 October 1996.

Failure to notify chargeability could lead to a penalty up to a maximum of the tax charged by assessments raised more than 12 months after the end of the year of assessment (again, mitigable by the Revenue). Notice was not required where tax had already been paid eg. under PAYE or by deduction at source and no further tax was payable.

3.9 Assessments

3.9.1 Introduction

In order that income tax was collected it had to be assessed (although there were special rules where there had been deduction of tax at source and for Schedule E). The inspector had to issue a statement (called a notice of assessment) showing the income subject to tax and the tax payable in relation to a *particular tax year*. A taxpayer could receive several assessments for a particular tax year, each relating to a different *source* of income taxable under a different *Schedule* or *Case*. The assessment was based on information received by the inspector in the return made by the taxpayer, or if no return had been received and the inspector believed there was a liability to tax, he issued an *estimated* assessment based on his judgement of the liability.

s.29

3.9.2 Time limits

The inspector had six years from the end of a particular fiscal year to issue or raise an assessment: an assessment relating to 1995/96 had to be issued by 5 April 2002. However, there were special rules where there has been *fraudulent or negligent conduct*. An assessment could then be raised at any time within the following 20 years. Thus if tax for 1995/96 had not been assessed, or had been under assessed, due to the *fraudulent or negligent conduct* (an undefined expression) of the taxpayer or someone acting on his behalf, an assessment could be raised up until 5 April 2016 to collect it. The Inspector did not need to obtain leave of a Commissioner to raise such an assessment outside the normal six year time limit.

s.34

If a taxpayer had died, assessments had to be raised within three years of the end of the tax year of death and, even in cases of fraudulent or negligent conduct, could only go back as far as tax years ending up to six years before death.

The rules on when a discovery assessment could be made (see 3.4.6) also applied under the old rules.

s.33

Where an assessment was excessive due to some *error or mistake* in the taxpayer's return or other statement supplied by him (eg. a set of accounts), the taxpayer could claim relief within six years of the end of the relevant tax year. The legislation covered errors of omission, mistakes arising from a failure to understand the law, and arithmetical errors. It did *not* cover failure on the part of the taxpayer to appeal against an assessment. It did not give relief where an assessment was settled on the grounds of *practice prevailing* if that practice was subsequently altered (eg. where a later tax case overturned an earlier interpretation of the law).

3.9.3 Appeals procedure

Once an assessment had been issued, the taxpayer must either have accepted it and paid the tax, or *appealed* against it if he considered it to be incorrect. The provisions were as follows:

s.31

(a)   the appeal must have been *in writing* and was made to the inspector;

(b)   it must have been made within *30 days* of the *issue* of the assessment; and

(c)   it must have been stated, in general terms, the grounds of appeal - eg. the assessment was considered to be excessive and not in accordance with draft accounts.

Appeals could be made after the 30 day limit had expired if the inspector was satisfied that:

(a)   there was a reasonable excuse; and

(b)   the application was made without undue delay.

The inspector must have given his consent to the late appeal in writing.

In many cases where the taxpayer appealed against an assessment, agreement was reached with the inspector informally. However, where agreement could not be reached, the appeal would be heard before either the General or Special Commissioners (see 1.3.2).

3.10   Payment of income tax and CGT

3.10.1 Introduction

Tax could be collected either at source (the taxpayer receiving income net of basic rate tax) or by an inspector's raising assessments for years up to and including 1995/96. The dates for payment of assessed income tax varied according to the schedule and case under which the income was assessable. There was also a due date for CGT (which was always collected by assessment).

3.10.2 Payment dates where tax is not postponed

Tax was due and payable on the *later* of:

(a)   the date provided in the legislation (commonly called the normal due   s.5 ICTA 1988
       date, or NDD); or

(b)   30 days after the date of issue of the assessment.

The normal due dates were as follows:

Income	Normal due date
Schedule A, Schedule D Cases III and IV and investment income under Schedule D Cases V and VI	1 January in the tax year
Schedule D Cases I and II and earned income under Schedule D Cases V and VI	Two equal instalments: (a) 1 January in the tax year (b) 1 July following the tax year
Schedule E	(a) During the tax year under PAYE (b) For additional tax due, 14 days after application by the collector
Income taxed at source	(a) Basic rate (lower rate for dividends): deducted at source during the tax year (b) Higher rate: 1 December following the tax year
Capital gains tax	1 December following the tax year (subject to instalment options) s.7 TCGA 1992

3.10.3 Postponement of tax

A taxpayer could seek to postpone tax if he believed that an assessment was excessive. If he appealed against an assessment he could, within the same 30 day time limit, apply to postpone all or part of the tax charged. Appealing and making a postponement application were separate matters, although they were usually dealt with at the same time. If a taxpayer only appealed, he had to pay the tax when it would have been due if there had been no appeal.

An application to postpone tax could be made outside the appeals time limit if the taxpayer's circumstances altered so as to give him grounds for believing that he had been overcharged.

The payment dates set out above always applied unless the taxpayer had postponed all or part of the tax charged by the assessment. When tax was postponed, the position was as follows.

For any remaining tax that the taxpayer had not applied to postpone, the due date for payment was the *later* of the normal due date and 30 days after the inspector agreed the postponement application.

When the appeal against the assessment was finally determined, some or all of the tax postponed might have turned out to be payable after all. Following determination of the appeal (whether by agreement with the inspector or by a decision of the Commissioners) the inspector issued a notice showing the total tax payable. Tax postponed was due for payment 30 days after the inspector issued this notice, except in the very unlikely event that the NDD was later (in that case the tax was due on the NDD).

Example

Jeremy received a 1994/95 Schedule D Case I assessment on 28 November 1994 showing tax payable of £12,000. He appealed against the assessment on 6 December 1994 and applied to postpone £4,000 of the tax charged. The inspector agreed to the postponement application on 18 December 1994. On 19 June 1995 the appeal was finally determined and the tax liability is agreed at £9,000.

When was the tax charged due for payment?

Solution

The tax not postponed was £8,000 (£12,000 - £4,000) and this was due for payment in two equal instalments of £4,000.

The first instalment was due on the later of: *Actual due date*

(a)	the NDD	1.1.95	
(b)	30 days after the agreement to postpone	17.1.95	17.1.95

The second instalment was due on the later of:

(a)	the NDD	1.7.95	1.7.95
(b)	30 days after the agreement to postpone	17.1.95	

The tax postponed that subsequently became payable, £1,000, was payable in two equal instalments of £500 each.

The first instalment was due on the later of: *Actual due date*

(a)	the NDD	1.1.95	
(b)	30 days after the appeal is finally determined	19.7.95	19.7.95

The second instalment was due on the later of:

(a)	the NDD	1.7.95	
(b)	30 days after the appeal was finally determined	19.7.95	19.7.95

If the final determination of the appeal lead to more tax being payable than was charged in the original assessment, the additional tax was be due for payment 30 days after the determination of the appeal, or on the NDD if this was later.

3.10.5 Repayments of tax

There was no particular time limit for the Inland Revenue to repay tax overpaid. Where a non-taxpayer received income net of tax, the Inland Revenue would consider a repayment claim during the year once the repayment due reached £50. Claims for repayments of any size could be made after the end of the year.

3.11 Interest on income tax and CGT paid late

3.11.1 Ordinary interest

s.86

Interest was charged on tax paid late. Interest (which was not tax-deductible) ran from the *reckonable date* to the day before payment was made.

Where either no appeal had been made, or an appeal had been made but there had been no application to postpone tax, the reckonable date was simply the date on which the tax should have been paid.

But where a postponement application had been made, the reckonable date was the middle date in order of time of:

(a)   the normal due date (or 30 days after issue of the assessment if it was issued later than the day 30 days before the NDD);

(b)   the actual due date (ADD);

(c)   the Table date.

The Table date depended on the type of income or gains, as follows.

Tax	Table date
Schedule A and Schedule D Cases I - VI	1 July 3 months after the end of the tax year (so 1 July 1995 for 1994/95)
Higher rate tax (where lower or basic rate deducted at source) and CGT	1 June 14 months after the end of the tax year (so 1 June 1996 for 1994/95)

The Table date was six months after the NDD (except for the second instalment of tax payable in two instalments, in which case it was the same date as the NDD for the second instalment).

Example

> Peter received a 1994/95 Schedule A assessment issued on 12 December 1994 showing tax payable of £30,000. He appealed against the assessment on 8 January 1995 and applied to postpone £5,000 of the tax charged. The inspector agreed to the postponement application on 29 January 1995. The appeal against the assessment was finally determined on 5 June 1995, and the tax payable was agreed to be £33,000. Peter paid tax of £25,000 on 1 April 1995 and a further £8,000 on 26 July 1995.
>
> **What interest on tax would he be liable to pay assuming a rate of 10% throughout?**

Solution

The first step was to separate the tax postponed and the tax not postponed (because the actual due dates are different).

Tax not postponed	*Tax postponed*
£25,000	£5,000

Then calculate each of the three dates.

(a)   later of: As for tax not postponed
    (i)   NDD (1.1.95); and
    (ii) 30 days after assessment
      (11.1.95): 11.1.95   11.1.95

(b)   ADD: later of: ADD: later of:
    (i)   NDD (1.1.95);   (i)   NDD (1.1.95);

    (ii) 30 days after agreement to   (ii) 30 days after determination of
      postpone (28.2.95):   appeal (5.7.95):
      28.2.95   5.7.95

(c)   Table date 1.7.95   1.7.95

The reckonable date was the middle one of the three.

28.2.95   1.7.95

Thus interest on tax was calculated as follows.

		£
(i)	On tax not postponed (28.2.95 -1.4.95):	
	£25,000 x 32/365 x 10%	219.18
(ii)	On tax postponed (1.7.95 - 26.7.95)	
	£5,000 x 25/365 x 10%	34.25
		253.43

Any tax not charged by the original assessment which subsequently became payable was treated as if it had been included in the original assessment and postponed, so interest ran from the same reckonable date as for tax postponed, in this case 1 July 1995. The interest was therefore £3,000 x 25/365 x 10% = £20.55

The total interest was £(253.43 + 20.55) = £273.98.

Example

Cynthia received a Schedule D Case I assessment for 1994/95, charging tax of £12,000. The assessment was issued on 1 February 1995. She applied to postpone all the tax, and the inspector agreed on 27 February 1995. The appeal was determined, with tax of £8,300 payable, on 1 September 1995 and Cynthia paid this amount on 20 September 1995. Interest on tax was at 10%. How much interest was payable?

Solution

	First instalment of £4,150	*Second instalment of £4,150*
NDD/30 days from issue	3.3.95	1.7.95
ADD	1.10.95	1.10.95
Table date	1.7.95	1.7.95
Reckonable date	1.7.95	1.7.95

Interest ran from 1 July to 20 September 1995 on both instalments, so interest was £8,300 x 81/365 x 10% = £184.19.

Certificates of tax deposit

A taxpayer might have wished to protect himself against interest on overdue tax. He could do this by purchasing a *certificate of tax deposit* which was then used to pay income tax and capital gains tax. The certificates carried interest which was payable gross and taxable in the hands of the taxpayer. The deposit could be used to pay tax at any time. When a deposit was used in this way the tax was treated as having been paid on the later of the normal due date for the tax and the date the deposit was made. Thus, provided the deposit was made before the normal due date, no charge to interest on overdue tax could arise. If the tax due was less than expected, unused certificates could be exchanged for cash.

3.11.2 Interest to make good a tax loss

Sometimes referred to as penalty interest, this was an alternative to ordinary interest. It could be imposed when an assessment had been made for the purpose of making good a loss of tax wholly or partly attributable to:

s.88

(a)   a failure to give a notice, make a return or produce or furnish a document or other information;

(b)   an error in any information, return, accounts or other document delivered to the Inland Revenue.

In common with ordinary interest on tax, penalty interest was not deductible in computing any tax liability. But, unlike ordinary interest, penalty interest ran from the normal due date for payment. Where penalty interest was charged on Schedule D Cases I and II tax, it ran on half of the tax from 1 January in the tax year and on the other half from 1 July following the tax year.

Penalty interest was likely to be imposed when a return was not sent back soon enough for the Revenue to assess income in time for tax to be payable by the normal due date (assuming of course that the return was not sent back within the 30 days allowed). For example, if a return was issued in April to a taxpayer who had taxed income on which he was liable to higher rate tax, and the return was not sent back until after 31 October, the Revenue might have charged penalty interest because they could not raise an assessment which would make the higher rate tax payable by the normal due date (1 December). However, penalty interest was not charged when no tax return was issued and the taxpayer supplied full details of income and gains within 12 months of the end of the tax year.

A taxpayer could not be charged both penalty interest and ordinary interest on tax on the same amount.

The Revenue must have served a 'notice of determination' on the taxpayer if penalty interest was to be imposed. Such a notice could be appealed against.

3.12 Repayment supplement on income tax and CGT

If a tax *repayment* was due to a taxpayer, because tax has been overpaid, then a tax free *repayment supplement* was added to the repayment due if the repayment was made more than 12 months after the end of the tax year to which the payment originally related. The taxpayer must have been resident in the UK or in another European Union state for the tax year for which the tax was paid.

s.824 ICTA 1988

s.283 TCGA 1992

Repayment supplement (RS) ran from 6 April following the date the tax was paid, except that it could not start to run until 12 months after the end of the tax year for which the tax was paid.

RS ran to the end of the tax month in which the repayment was made. A tax month ran from the 6th of one month to the 5th of the next.

Example

Jones pays Schedule A tax relating to 1994/95 as follows:

Date paid	Amount £
1 January 1995	2,000
1 August 1995	1,500
1 May 1996	1,000

Following a claim for loss relief a repayment of £3,000 was made on 21 July 1996.

What repayment supplement was added to the repayment assuming an interest rate of 10%?

Solution

The repayment was deemed to be made up of the latest paid tax first. In this example the £3,000 was made up as follows.

£	Date paid	Date from which RS runs
1,000	1 May 1996	6 April 1997
1,500	1 August 1995	6 April 1996
500	1 January 1995	6 April 1996
3,000		

The repayment was made on 21 July 1996. Repayment supplement was calculated as follows.

£1,000 paid on 1 May 1996: no RS.

£1,500 paid on 1 August 1995: RS from 6 April 1996 to 5 August 1996.

£500 paid on 1 January 1995: RS from 6 April 1996 to 5 August 1996.

Therefore the RS was £(1,500 + 500) x 10% x 4/12 = £66.67

QUESTIONS

1. In a case where a taxpayer has income which has not been charged to tax, the onus is on the Inland Revenue to discover that an amount of tax is due. TRUE/FALSE?

2. What are the due filing dates for tax returns for 1996/97?

3. How will 1996/97 payments on account be calculated?

4. A tax return for 1997/98 is issued in April 1997 and filed in May 1998 at the same time paying the final income tax due. What charges will be made on the taxpayer?

5. An assessment is issued to Humphrey on 12 November 1995, showing Schedule D Case VI investment income for 1995/96 of £8,000, tax due £2,000. Humphrey estimates that his Schedule D Case VI income for the year will not exceed £5,000.

    (a) What will happen if Humphrey fails to take any action in relation to the assessment?

    (b) What action should Humphrey take?

6. What would be the situation in question 4(b) above if Humphrey had not received the notice of assessment until 5 January 1996, it having been delayed in the Christmas post?

7. Gerald receives bank interest of £6,000 (net) during 1995/96. Gerald is a higher rate taxpayer, having substantial employment income. When is the higher rate tax on his bank interest due for payment?

8. Explain briefly the significance of the "Table date" given by s.86 TMA 1970.

SOLUTIONS

1. FALSE - the onus is on the taxpayer to inform the Inland Revenue (3.3).

2. Self assessment   -   31 January 1998, or 3 months after issue if later.

    Other returns   -   30 September 1997, or 2 months after issue if later.

    (3.4.1)

3. 31.1.97   -   Schedule A & D payment made on 1.1.96

    31.7.97   -   Schedule DI/II payment made on 1.7.96

    (3.5.2)

4. £100 for filing within 6 months after the 31 January 1998 filing date.

    Surcharge of 5% of tax due being paid over 28 days late.

    Interest from 31 January 1998 until day before date tax paid. Interest on surcharge if paid more than 30 days after imposed.

    (3.4.2, 3.6.1, 3.6.2)

5. (a)   The assessment will become final in the sum of £8,000; the tax due of £2,000 is payable by 1 January 1996 to avoid a charge to interest on overdue tax.

    (b)   Humphrey should :

    (i)   appeal against the assessment by 12 December 1995; and

    (ii)   apply for postponement of payment of (£8,000 - 5,000) x 25% = £750, leaving £1,250 to pay (on the later of 1 January 1996 and 30 days after the Inspector's agreement to the postponement application).

    (3.9.3, 3.10.2, 3.10.3 and 3.11.1).

6. Humphrey would have to ask the inspector to exercise his discretion in accepting an appeal made outside the normal 30-day time limit (3.9.3).

7. On the later of:

    (a)   1 December 1996; or

    (b)   30 days after the issue of an assessment

    (3.10.2).

8. The significance of the Table date is that, so long as an assessment has been raised, interest will commence to run from the Table date on any tax unpaid by that date, even if the actual due date has not yet been reached (3.11.1).

```
┌─────────────────────────────────────────┐
│            SESSION 4                      │
│                                           │
│   INCOME FROM LAND AND                    │
│        BUILDINGS                          │
│                                           │
└─────────────────────────────────────────┘
```

The purpose of this session is to set out the Schedule A rules on the taxation of income from land and buildings.

References: ICTA 1988 unless otherwise stated.

4.1   Schedule A

4.1.1 Introduction

In preparation for the self-assessment regime, the income tax rules for the taxation of income from land were radically simplified for 1995/96 onwards. The changes came in a year ahead of self-assessment to avoid concentrating too many simplification measures in one year.

However, the land taxation rules that applied for individuals up to and including 1994/95 are still applicable for companies receiving income from land and will be explained in your Corporation Tax study text. Note therefore that there are two versions of s.15 ICTA 1988 - one for income tax as referred to in this session and one for corporation tax.

Under the old rules - still applying for companies - rents were assessable on a receivable basis, expenses were generally relieved when paid and there were restrictions on the set-off of losses and profits from different types of leases. There were also distinctions between furnished lettings - assessed under Schedule D VI - and unfurnished lettings - assessed under Schedule A.

Under the new rules all letting by an individual landlord is treated as a single "Schedule A business" with the profit or loss computed for a tax year on the normal business accounting principles - ie. rents and expenses included on an accruals basis.

Schedule A applies whether the property is furnished or unfurnished and no distinction is made between types of leases. As all letting is a single business, profits and losses on individual properties are automatically set-off.

Note that a Schedule A 'business' is defined in very wide terms effectively as any business carried on (or transaction entered into) "for the exploitation as a source of rents or other receipts of any estate, interest or rights in or over land in the United Kingdom".

s.15

4.1.2 Definition of Schedule A income

The Schedule A charge for individuals for 1995/96 onwards is based on the annual profits or gains arising from the business; including:

-       receipts in respect of licences to occupy/use land and the exercise of rights over land;

-       rent charges, ground annuals, feu duties and any other annual payments reserved, etc. in respect of land;

- income for the use of fixed caravans and permanently moored houseboats;

- sums receivable for the use of furniture provided in respect of premises producing Schedule A income.

Other income from property is also brought into the new Schedule A income tax charge; e.g. the taxable element of lease premiums, sums received on the assignment of a lease granted at an undervalue, and receipts from the sale of land with a right to reconveyance.

s.34
s.35

s.36

4.1.3 Computation of amounts chargeable under Schedule A

s.21

For 1995/96 onwards the income tax charge under Schedule A on the person receiving or entitled to the income is computed by reference to the full amount of the profits or gains arising in the year of assessment.

The basic principle is that such profits or gains (and any losses) are computed as if the Schedule A business were a trade taxed under Schedule D Case I and normal accounting policies (including the accruals concept) are to be used. This applies subject to any express provision to the contrary in the Income Tax Acts. Note that the income is assessable as investment income under Schedule A and is not actually turned into trading income; thus, there remains an important distinction between a business and a trade.

Before 1995/96 the set off of expenses was restricted to certain categories such as the cost of repairing and managing the let property. Also there were restrictions on relief for bad debts, relief for losses on properties let at a nominal rent and relief for expenses incurred when the property was empty. These are dealt with under the new rules as follows:

(a) Expenses are allowed if they are wholly and exclusively incurred for the "business" of letting on Schedule D Case I principles. This makes little practical difference since virtually all such expenses (eg. advertising, accountancy and insurance) would have been allowed under the old rules. A number of types of trading expense are disallowed under Schedule D Case I such as business entertaining and depreciation (for which capital allowances are given instead). The details are covered in your Business Income Tax study text.

(b) However, bad debts were only allowed if rent had been waived to avoid hardship or if efforts had been made to enforce payment. Under the new rules bad debts are allowed on business principles so if a rent payment appears unlikely the landlord can provide for it in his letting accounts at the end of the tax year.

(c) Capital allowances are not allowed on furniture used in a dwelling. Instead, the Revenue give relief for such capital expenditure but only on a renewals basis. The original cost and the cost of any improvements are not relieved but the cost of replacing furniture to the same standard is allowed as an expense. As this is cumbersome to administer, for furnished lettings there was a concession whereby an amount equal to 10% of rents (net of certain expenses such as water rates and council tax if paid by the landlord) was allowed as a deduction in place of claiming relief for the replacement of furniture. This concession also applies under the new rules. The cost of repairing or maintaining furniture and fittings is also allowed whether the renewals basis or the 10% relief is claimed.

(d)   Property may be let at a nominal or "peppercorn" rent perhaps to an elderly relative. Under the old rules any profit was chargeable but any loss could only be carried forward against profits under the same lease. Under the new rules all letting is a single business so such losses would be automatically relieved. However, the landlord's expenses incurred on a nominal letting property are arguably not "wholly and exclusively for the trade" and the Revenue are likely to restrict the expense deducted.

(e)   If there is a business of letting, the landlord can set-off the running expenses incurred on empty properties against property income generally. Under the old rules expenses were generally only allowed where the property was empty between commercial lettings or between purchase and first commercial let.

(f)   If property normally let furnished is occupied at some time by the owner, the allowable deduction for repairs, insurance, council tax and so on is restricted to a proportion based on the period that the property is available for letting. For example, if the Revenue accepted that letting took place throughout the year and was occupied by the owner for 4 weeks and by tenants for 30 weeks, 48/52 of the expenses would be allowed. Expenses specific to the letting such as advertising would be allowed in full. This treatment is not altered by the change to the new rules.

As Schedule D I computation principles apply, both loan interest and overdraft interest are deductible in computing Schedule A income for income tax purposes with effect from 6 April 1995, provided the related borrowing was applied wholly and exclusively for the purposes of the Schedule A business.

s.375A

Where interest is both allowable as a deduction under Schedule A and eligible for MIRAS relief, the taxpayer can give notice to the Inland Revenue to take the loan out of MIRAS from a specified date. Such a notice is irrevocable, must be given within 22 months from the end of the tax year in which it is first to take effect, and remains in force until the Schedule A business is permanently discontinued. Only then can the loan be reinstated within the MIRAS scheme.

Where a Schedule A business is permanently discontinued, the Schedule D Case I & II rules on post-cessation receipts and expenditure will apply (see Business Tax study text).

4.1.4 Capital allowances

For 1995/96 onwards capital allowances in respect of the items shown below are to be deducted (and balancing charges added) in computing the income of a Schedule A business as though it were a trade set up and commenced on or after 6 April 1995. The assets to which this treatment applies are:

(a)   machinery or plant used for the maintenance, repair or management of premises producing Schedule A income.

(b)   machinery or plant let (eg. as part of a building) otherwise than by way of trade.

CAA 1990 s.61

(c)   expenditure on thermal insulation of an industrial building, etc.

CAA 1990 s.67

Capital allowances are explained in detail in the Business Income Tax study text. However, in outline all such qualifying expenditure on plant and machinery attracts a 25% writing down allowance computed on a reducing balance basis starting in the tax year of expenditure.

As explained above, capital allowances are not available in respect of plant or machinery let in a dwelling house, and the renewals basis or the wear and tear allowances (normally 10% of rents) for furnished lettings is continued.

4.1.5 Schedule A losses

Where there is a Schedule A loss for 1995/96 and subsequent years:

(a)   The general rule is that the loss is to be carried forward and set against the Schedule A income for the following year (and subsequent years insofar as not relieved in the next following year).

s.379A

(b)   Losses resulting from capital allowances treated as a Schedule A expense may be relieved against the taxpayer's general income for the year of the loss and the next following tax year.

The loss relief at (a) above is automatic and no claim is required. Losses under (b) above must be claimed within two years of the end of the year in which the loss is incurred (this time limit reducing to 12 months from the self assessment filing date for the year of the loss.

4.1.6   Premiums on leases

When a premium or similar consideration is received on the *grant* (that is, by a landlord to a tenant) of a short lease (50 years or less), part of the premium is treated as rent and is thus taxed under Schedule A in the year of grant. A lease is considered to end on the date when it is most likely to terminate.

s.34

The premium taxed under Schedule A is the whole premium, less 2% of the premium for each complete year of the lease, except the first year. This is expressed as the formula:

Premium	£A
Less: 2% (n - 1) x A	(a)
Schedule A assessment	£X

This rule does not apply on the *assignment* of a lease (one tenant selling his entire interest in the property to another).

Premiums paid by traders

Where a trader (assessed under Schedule D Case I or II) pays a premium for a lease he may deduct an amount from his taxable profits in each year of the lease. The amount deductible is the figure assessed on the landlord divided by the number of years of the lease. For example, suppose that B, a trader, pays A a premium of £30,000 for a ten year lease. A is assessed under Schedule A on £30,000 - (£30,000 x (10 - 1) x 2%) = £24,600. B can therefore deduct £24,600/10 = £2,460 in each of the ten years. He starts with the accounts year in which the lease starts and apportions the relief to the nearest month.

s.87

Premiums for granting subleases

A tenant may decide to sublet property and to charge a premium on the grant of a lease to the subtenant. This premium is taxed under Schedule A in the normal way (because this is a grant and not an assignment, the original tenant is retaining an interest in the property), except that where the tenant originally paid a premium for his own head lease a relief is given, computed as:

$$\text{Taxable premium for head lease} \times \frac{\text{duration of sub-lease}}{\text{duration of head lease}}$$

Example

C granted a lease to D on 1 March 1986 for a period of 40 years. D paid a premium of £16,000. On 1 June 1996 D granted a sublease to E for a period of ten years. E paid a premium of £30,000. Calculate the amount assessable under Schedule A for 1996/97 in respect of the premium received by D.

Solution

	£
Premium received by D	30,000
Less: £30,000 x 2% x (10 - 1)	(5,400)
	24,600
Less: allowance for premium paid	
(£16,000 - (£16,000 x 39 x 2%)) x 10/40	(880)
Amount assessable	£23,720

4.1.7 Furnished holiday lettings

A small hotel, or bed and breakfast accommodation, may be taxed as a trade under Schedule D Case I. Expenses may then be computed according to Schedule D Case I rules, profits are 'earned' income and losses may be relieved against other income.

As we have seen, furnished lettings are assessable under Schedule A as part of a taxpayer's 'business' of letting and relief for losses is therefore more restricted. Also the income is not treated as earned.

The fine line between a Schedule DI trade and a Schedule A business of letting is a matter of interpretation and usually depends on other services, such as meals, being provided in addition to accommodation.

There are special rules designed to ease the tax position of holiday lettings. Provided certain conditions are satisfied the income from such lettings is assessed under Schedule A but Schedule D Case I rules apply to individuals for all purposes, as follows.

s.503

(a) Relief for losses is available as if they were trading losses, including the facility to set losses against other income

(b) The income qualifies as net relevant earnings for retirement annuity and personal pension relief

(c) Profits are treated as earned income

(d) Capital allowances are available as for traders

(e) Capital gains tax rollover relief, retirement relief, relief for gifts of business assets and relief for loans to traders are all available

The letting must be of furnished accommodation made on a commercial basis with a view to the realisation of profit. The property must satisfy the following conditions.

s.504

(a) It is available for commercial letting to the public for not less than 140 days in a year of assessment and is so let for at least 70 days in that 140 day period. If two or more properties each pass the 140 day test separately, then they need only pass the 70 day test on average. That is, the test becomes [(sum of numbers of days let)/(number of properties)] must be at least 70. A landlord may choose to leave particular properties out of the averaging computation if they would pull the average down to below 70 days.

(b)   For at least seven months in the year of assessment (including the 70 days) it is not normally in the same occupation for more than 31 days.

Where the taxpayer also has other letting income he is treated as running a 'business of letting' and a 'business of furnished holiday letting' and the two are computed quite separately.

4.1.8 The rent a room scheme

If an individual lets a room or rooms, furnished, in his main residence and the income from the letting would be assessable under Schedule A (or Schedule D Case I), then a special exemption may apply.

ss.59 and Sch 10
F(No.2)A 1992

The limit on the exemption is gross rents (before any expenses or capital allowances) of £3,250 a year. This limit is halved if any other person (including the first person's spouse) also received income from renting accommodation in the property while the property was the first person's main residence.

If gross rents (plus balancing charges arising because of capital allowances in earlier years) are not more than the limit, the rents (and balancing charges) are wholly exempt from income tax and expenses and capital allowances are ignored. However, the taxpayer may claim to ignore the exemption, for example to generate a loss by taking into account both rent and expenses.

If gross rents exceed the limit, the taxpayer will be taxed in the ordinary way, ignoring the rent a room scheme, unless he elects for the 'alternative basis'. If he so elects, he will be taxable on gross receipts plus balancing charges less £3,250 (or £1,625 if the limit is halved), with no deductions for expenses or capital allowances.

An election to ignore the exemption or an election for the alternative basis must be made within one year of the end of the year of assessment concerned. An election to ignore the exemption applies only for the year for which it is made, but an election for the alternative basis remains in force until it is withdrawn or until a year in which gross rents do not exceed the limit.

4.1.9 Deduction of tax from payments to non-residents

For 1996/97 onwards the existing provisions of ICTA 1988 section 43 - under which tenants are required to deduct tax from payments made direct to non-resident landlords and under which property agents may be taxed on behalf of such landlords - are repealed. From 6 April 1996 regulations provide for:

s.42A

(a)   Tax to be deducted at source from income paid to non-residents from property in the UK. Such deduction at source will be made by the agent for the property or (where there is no agent) by the tenant. There will then be a final settling up with the non-resident under self-assessment

(b)   For rent, etc. to be paid gross to the non-resident where he chooses, by agreement with the Inland Revenue, to include tax on income from property in the payments on account which he makes under self-assessment

4.1.10 Income from overseas property

For 1995/96 onwards the income tax treatment under Schedule D Case V of income from property situated outside the UK is aligned with the new Schedule A rules. In outline, the main changes are:

(a)   All income arising from overseas property - even if in different countries - is to be treated as derived from a single Schedule A business which is separate and distinct from any Schedule A business carried on by the taxpayer in the UK. Therefore, there will be no possibility of obtaining relief for a UK Schedule A loss against overseas rental income, or *vice versa*. [NB: For 1995/96 and 1996/97 only each separate overseas property is treated as a single business and as the only such business carried on by the taxpayer.]

(b)   Income from overseas property will continue to be assessed under Schedule D Case V, but the assessable amount is to be computed using the new Schedule A rules.

The above provisions do not apply to foreign domiciliaries (or to Commonwealth citizens or citizens of the Republic of Ireland who are not ordinarily resident in the UK) assessable on the remittance basis.

QUESTIONS

1. David buys his first property for letting on 1 August 1996 and grants a tenancy to Ethel from 1 December 1996 at £3,600 pa. payable quarterly in advance. How much is assessable in 1996/97?

2. Paul grants a lease for 10 years to Graham for a premium of £20,000. How much is assessable as rent and when will it be assessed?

3. Catherine rents out five furnished properties at £1,600 pa. each and pays the water rates of £320 pa. on each. Assuming the renewals basis is not claimed, how will relief for wear and tear of furnishings will be given?

4. John pays insurance premiums for 12 months in advance on 1 October each year to cover the structure of all his letting properties. He pays £4,800 in 1995 and £5,200 in 1996. How much would be allowed against his Schedule A business income for 1996/97?

5. Debbie lets a flat to her widowed mother for £600 pa. when a market rent would be £3,600 pa. Debbie pays all the letting expenses which amount to £1,800 for 1996/97. How are these figures reflected in her 1996/97 Schedule A profits?

6. Fred has let three holiday bungalows during 1996/97 making a net loss. Explain briefly the difference in treating this loss should the lettings count as furnished holiday lettings. (No capital allowances are involved.)

7. Where profits are being made what is the main income tax advantage of a 'furnished holiday letting' Schedule A business?

SOLUTIONS

1. Schedule A 1996/97 - rent earned 1.12.96 - 5.4.97 ie. 4/12 x £3,600 = £1,200.
    (4.1.3)

	£
2. Premium	20,000
Less: £20,000 x 2% x (10 - 1)	(3,600)
Schedule A	£16,400

    Assessable in the year the lease is granted. (4.1.6)

3. Wear and tear allowance against rents:

    5 x (1,600 - 320) x 10% = £640   (4.1.3)

4. Insurance premiums accrued in 1996/97.

	£
6/12 x £4,800	2,400
6/12 x £5,200	2,600
	£5,000 (4.1.3)

5. Revenue are likely to argue that as only $(\frac{600}{3,600})$ 1/6 of a market rent is charged, only 1/6 of the expenses: £300 will be allowed as wholly and exclusively incurred. (4.1.3)

6. Schedule A losses are generally carried forward against Schedule A profits. However if they arise from FHL they are allowed (under s.380 ICTA 1988) against STI. (4.1.5 and 4.1.7)

7. FHL Schedule A income is treated as earned income (other Schedule A income is investment income). Primarily this allows the rents to provide relief for PPS (and RAS) contributions.   (4.1.7)

The purpose of this session is to:

- describe the income chargeable and bases of assessment under Schedule D Case III and Schedule D Case VI

- describe the treatment of specific important financial investments

- outline some major anti-avoidance rules relating to investments

- set out the rules on tax exempt special savings accounts, personal equity plans and the enterprise investment scheme

- describe the tax treatment of pensions and the tax relief available for contributions to both employers' and personal pension schemes

- describe the tax treatment of both qualifying and non-qualifying life assurance policies

References: ICTA 1988 unless otherwise stated.

5.1 Schedule D Case III

5.1.1 Introduction

Schedule D Case III is principally concerned with untaxed interest, ie. interest not taxed at source. The income assessed is the full amount arising without any deductions for expenses. Examples are interest on: s.18(3) s.64

(a) loans between individuals

(b) certain government stocks, notably $3^1/2\%$ War Loan

(c) National Savings Bank accounts. The first £70 on *ordinary* accounts at the National Savings Bank is exempt   s.325

(d) quoted Eurobonds   s.124

(e) certificates of tax deposit

Maintenance payments under pre 15 March 1988 UK court orders to former or separated spouses or children under 21, or to any person for the maintenance of a child under 21, are assessable under Schedule D Case III to the extent that they are taxable at all (see 2.6.7).

Individuals who are not liable to income tax (eg. because their allowances cover their income) can certify their status (on Form R85) to any bank or building society at which they have a deposit account and interest will be credited gross. Should the income prove to be assessable, the individual must declare it in the usual way and tax will be paid under self assessment.

Schedule D Case III is also used to tax discounts, including discounts on Treasury Bills.

The rules for Schedule D Case III have been changed to facilitate self-assessment, and we must distinguish between two types of sources of income.

(a)   *New sources* are those where income first arose after 5 April 1994 (even if the investments were made earlier).

(b)   Old *sources* are those where income first arose before 6 April 1994.

From 1997/98, the rules for new sources will also apply to old sources. There are special rules for the transitional year 1996/97.

s.64

5.1.2   Basis of assessment for old sources

The income assessed in each tax year is that arising in the preceding tax year. For example, income arising during the year to 5 April 1995 is assessed in 1995/96. See 5.1.6 below for the basis of assessment in 1996/97, the transitional year.

s.64

Special rules apply in opening and closing years.

(a)   In the first tax year *in which income arises,* the actual income arising in that year is assessed.

s.66

(b)   In the second year the actual income arising in that second year is assessed, unless the first income arose on 6 April in the first year: in that case the preceding year basis applies to the second year.

s.66

(c)   In the third year the preceding year basis applies: income of the second year is assessed. However, the taxpayer can elect (for the third year only) to be assessed on the income arising in that third year. Notice of the election is required in writing within six years of the end of the year for which it applies. If income first arose on 6 April, this election for actual basis is available for the second year instead of the third year.

s.66

(d)   In the year the *source* ceases to be owned (the year the account is closed or the securities are sold) the actual income of that year is assessed.

s.67

(e)   The penultimate year is assessed on a preceding year basis but the Revenue can revise this to an actual basis.

s.67

(f)   The rules in d) and (e) continue to apply to an old source ceasing before 6 April 1998 so they are still relevant for exam purposes.

para 5 Sch 20FA 1994

If no income arises from a source for six consecutive years the taxpayer may (within two years from the end of the six years) claim to treat the source as having ceased when income last arose. If income later arises and such a claim has been made, the income will be treated as arising from a fresh source.

Example

An account yields the following interest until closed on 30 June 1997.

	£
1 January 1995	630
1 January 1996	420
1 January 1997	500
30 June 1997	230

What would be the Schedule D Case III assessments for all the years affected?

Solution

	£
1995/96 (Antepenultimate year)	
PYB	630
1996/97 (Penultimate year)	
PYB (original assessment) £420	
Actual £500	
The Revenue would revise to actual	500
1997/98 (Final year)	
Actual	230

5.1.3 Changes in sources

If the taxpayer acquires a new source of income, the commencement provisions apply to the income from that source. Indeed, a major change in an existing source can be treated by the Revenue as a new source following a case where a new source was held to exist when a taxpayer added a large sum to an existing deposit account. In practice, no adjustment is made unless a deposit or withdrawal is substantial. For examination purposes any material change in interest not explicable by changes in interest rates should be treated as indicating a new source. If this change occurs after 5 April 1994 see 5.1.5 below.

s.66(3)

Hart v Sangster (1957)

5.1.4 Spouses

Where a husband and wife are living together and one has an old source of Schedule D Case III income which wholly passes to the other on the first spouse's death, the preceding year basis continues undisturbed unless the personal representatives or the survivor ask for the cessation rules to be applied.

ESC A7

5.1.5 Basis of assessment for new sources

For sources where income first arises after 5 April 1994 the current year basis applies. The amount of income assessable for a tax year is the amount arising in that year. Income arises when it is paid or credited: accrued income not yet paid or credited is ignored. The old PYB rules are irrelevant.

5.1.6 Transitional rules for 1996/97

For a source on which income first arose before 6 April 1994 the transitional rules provide for a notional amount of Schedule D Case III income to be assessed in 1996/97, prior to the current year basis applying for 1997/98 onwards.

The amount assessed in 1996/97 will be 50% of the income *arising* in 1995/96 and 1996/97.

Example

Gladys receives the following amounts of interest on her NSB investment account:

December 1994	£2,000
December 1995	£2,300
December 1996	£2,700
December 1997	£3,000

You are required to calculate the assessments for all years.

Solution

1995/96	(PYB)	£2.000
1996/97	(Transitional year)	
	- 50% x (2,300 + 2,700)	£2.500
1997/98	(CYB)	£3.000

If 1995/96 is assessed on an actual basis, due to, for example, the election being made for this in the third year, then 1996/97 will also be assessed on an actual basis.

Special anti avoidance rules prevent taxpayers from taking advantage of the transitional rules to increase the amount of income which drops out of charge in 1996/97.

para 9 Sch 22 FA 1995

5.2   Schedule D Case VI

This case deals with 'any annual profits or gains not falling under any other Case of Schedule D and not charged by virtue of Schedule A or E'.

s.18

Examples are income or profits from:

(a)   The sale of patent rights

(b)   Certain 'post cessation' receipts after a trade has ceased

(c)   Casual commission (eg. on arranging insurance)

(d)   Balancing charges on a lessor of industrial buildings (see Business Taxation study text)

(e)   Receipts from casual authorship

(f)   'Interest elements' taxed under the accrued interest scheme (refer to paragraph 5.4.1 below)

The basis of assessment has always been the actual gains or profits arising in the year of assessment. This basis also applies under the CYB rules so no adjustments or transitional provisions are required.

s.69

5.3   Taxation of income from other investments

5.3.1   Tax-free investments

The proceeds of National Savings Certificates (including indexed-linked issues), SAYE (building society, bank, or National Savings schemes) and Premium Bond winnings are all tax-free. The first £70 pa. interest from a National Savings Bank Ordinary Account held by an individual is also tax-free.

s.326
s.325

Interest and bonuses on TESSAs (tax exempt special savings accounts) (see section 5.5 below), income from a PEP (Personal equity plan) (see section 5.6 below) and dividends from VCTs (Venture Capital Trusts) (see section 5.8 below) are tax-free.

s.326A

5.3.2   Bank or building society interest

Most building society and bank deposit interest is paid net of lower rate tax, but this tax is refundable to individuals if it exceeds their tax liability. There are arrangements under which individuals who are not liable to tax may, by providing a certificate, receive their interest gross.

ss.477, 480A

Both building societies and banks offer higher rates of interest to investors who have a large lump sum to invest or who are prepared to give a longer period of notice for withdrawals. Note that interest on qualifying time deposits (ie. £50,000+ invested for specified terms of not more than 5 years) is paid gross. They may also pay interest gross on certificates of deposit for at least £50,000 with terms of up to five years. This interest is assessed under Schedule D Case III on a current year basis.

ss.481(5), 482(6)

National Savings Bank interest is paid gross for whatever amount deposited and taxed under Schedule D Case III.

5.3.3   National Savings Certificates

These are attractive particularly to higher rate taxpayers as the accumulated interest paid at the end of the period of investment is totally free from income tax and CGT. Not surprisingly, there is a maximum holding permitted (£10,000 for the 42nd issue - with holders of previous matured issues being able to reinvest an additional £20,000 (max)). The investment earns compound interest at 5.85% p.a. (currently) if held for a maximum period of five years.

Depending on your views of likely future inflation levels, National Savings Indexed-Linked Certificates may be more attractive to higher rate taxpayers. The maximum holding of 8th issue certificates is £10,000, and, provided they are held for one year, the repayment value is equal to the original purchase price plus an amount based on the rise in the RPI since the month of purchase, plus compound interest at the rate of 3% of the purchase price if they are held for five years.

As far as the examination is concerned this detail is less important than the general idea of advising a higher-rate taxpayer anticipating high levels of inflation that National Savings Indexed-Linked Certificates may be a good investment.

5.3.4   Save As You Earn (SAYE)

SAYE schemes, offered by building societies, banks, and through National Savings, provided a means of regular saving with a tax-free return at the end of a fixed term, usually five to seven years. Under the National Savings Yearly Plan, investors save a regular sum of up to £400 per month for one year. At the end of the year these savings are used to purchase a Yearly Plan Savings Certificate which earns a guaranteed return, tax free, over four years. Both the monthly savings and certificates earn a lower guaranteed rate, still tax-free, over shorter periods.

With effect from 1 December 1994, new schemes are not available unless linked to an employee share option scheme. Ordinary SAYE schemes certified prior to 1 December 1994 are not affected.

5.3.5   Local authority bonds

Otherwise known as yearling bonds, these are lump sum investments (£1,000 minimum) for between one and five years. However, they can be readily sold if necessary. Interest is payable half-yearly under deduction of lower rate tax. The attraction of these bonds lies in the competitive rates offered as local authorities seek to satisfy short-term borrowing requirements.

It is possible to hold small quantities of yearling bonds and sell them 'cum-interest' on the stock market and effectively convert the accrued interest into a capital gain. Provided the nominal value of fixed interest securities held at any time does not exceed £5,000 the accrued income scheme (see 5.4.1 below) does not affect such transactions.

5.3.6   Government securities

Government or gilt-edged securities ('gilts') carry a wide range of fixed interest rates, and some of the more recent issues link both the interest and the capital repayment to the RPI. Interest is paid under deduction of lower rate tax, with the exception of $3^1/_2\%$ War Loan. However, some gilts can alternatively be acquired through the National Savings Stock Register, when interest is always paid gross. In either case, interest is fully taxable at the lower rate in the recipient's hands.

Most gilts have a redemption date upon which the nominal value will be paid to the holder. Thus, stocks purchased at a discount carry a guaranteed capital gain if held to redemption. In the meantime the market price will fluctuate. Any gain on disposal or redemption is free of capital gains tax for individuals.

As with yearling bonds, gilts have scope for converting interest into capital if sold 'cum interest', but subject to the same anti-avoidance rules.

5.3.7   Unit trusts

A unit trust allocates units to investors in return for the money they pay in. The sums paid in are then invested in shares and securities. The dividends and interest arising on those shares and securities are passed on to the investors. When an investor wishes to withdraw his investment, he usually sells his units back to the unit trust managers. The price of units varies with the market value of the shares and securities, so investors may make gains or losses.

If a unit trust invests in shares, then a distribution of dividend income to an investor is taxed on the investor in the same way as a dividend from a company: it is grossed up by multiplying by 100/80, and if it falls within the basic rate band it is only taxed at 20%. Credit is given for the 20% tax already suffered.   s.468

If a unit trust invests in securities yielding interest, the interest received is paid out to investors net of lower rate tax. It is taxed on the investors in exactly the same way as any other interest received net. It is grossed up by multiplying by 100/80 and credit is given for the 20% tax already suffered.   s.468L

5.4 Anti-Avoidance

5.4.1 Accrued income scheme - bond washing

ss.710-728

In the past, taxpayers sought to convert income into capital, for example by the process known as bond washing. Bond washing involves selling securities cum interest (ie. with the right to receive the next interest payment) normally just prior to the ex interest date. The proceeds received would include an element for the interest payment sold. Hence the proceeds would, without special provision, be categorised entirely as capital, despite the fact that they reflect the interest accrued, but unpaid, up to the date of transfer. In the case of government securities ("gilts") and most UK company debentures no chargeable gain can arise on a disposal by an individual and there may therefore be an advantage in realising income (taxable at up to 40%) in a capital form.

To prevent this form of tax avoidance, for transfers of securities (eg. gilts, debentures, loan stock etc. but not shares in a company), the "accrued income scheme" applies. In essence, on a *cum interest* transfer, the transferor is treated as realising income equal to the interest accrued up to the settlement date for the transfer. Such deemed income is assessed under Schedule D Case VI. The transferee is treated as entitled to relief of a similar amount, normally given by deduction from the next interest payment he receives.

In the case of an *ex interest* transfer (where the *transferor* will receive the whole of the next interest payment) similar, but opposite, adjustments will be made, so that the transferee is charged to tax under Schedule D Case VI in respect of the interest accruing from the settlement date of the transfer up to the next interest payment date. The transferor, on the other hand, is entitled to relief of an identical amount, given by deduction from the interest payment he receives.

The rules do not apply in a number of situations, principally where an individual has not held securities exceeding £5,000 (nominal value) in the current or preceding year of assessment.

Example

Ralph purchases £10,000 5% Treasury Stock cum interest, on 1 February 1996, and sells it cum interest on 1 April 1997. Interest is paid on the stock on 1 May and 1 November each year.

The assessable income for 1996/97 is:

		£
1.5.96	Interest - 5% x £10,000 x $^6/_{12}$	250
	Less: accrued income relief	
	- 5% x £10,000 x $^3/_{12}$	(125)
		125
1.11.96	Interest - 5% x £10,000 x $^6/_{12}$	250
		£375
1.4.97	Accrued income	
	- 5% x £10,000 x $^5/_{12}$	£208

5.4.2 Deep discounted and deep gain stock

Another technique used to convert income into capital gains was when a company issued 'deep discounted stock'. The stock would have a low coupon (interest) rate but be issued at a deep (ie. large) discount to its nominal value to compensate the investor. On a sale before redemption, no charge to income tax arose on the discount element. This loophole is covered by treating the discount as interest accruing over the life of the security on a compound basis. The proportion of the discount accruing in each 'income period' - the 'income element' - is ascertained, and in the year when the stock is sold the individual will be assessed under Schedule D Case III for the aggregate income elements accruing in the period of ownership. The issuing company obtains tax relief on the income element arising in each corporation tax accounting period. The definition of 'deep discount security' includes securities issued at a deep discount by governments, public or local authorities of the UK or any other country.

s.57 & Sch 4

The deep discount security legislation was found to be lacking, in the sense that a security issued apparently at a deep discount, but with some variable feature (eg. variable interest rate or redemption date) fell outside the scope of the rules outlined above. Accordingly, a new type of security - a "deep gain security" - was identified. On disposal or redemption of a deep gain security, the whole of the excess of proceeds over acquisition cost will be charged to income tax under Schedule D Case III.

FA 1989 s.94 & Sch 11

5.4.3 Offshore funds

Investors might also try to convert income into capital gains by investing in offshore roll up funds (eg. overseas resident unit trusts). These funds, usually based in tax havens to minimise their own taxation, invest typically in income bearing financial instruments held in sterling or other currencies. This income is rolled up in the fund (ie. deliberately not paid out to investors) and without special legislation would be taxed as a capital gain, subject only to CGT, when the investment in the fund was realised by the UK investor.

ss.757-764

To prevent this, there is a charge to income tax under Schedule D Case VI on a gain ("the offshore income gain") realised on a disposal of an interest in an offshore fund (eg. disposal of units in a non-resident unit trust). This applies if the fund is or has been a non-qualifying offshore fund. A qualifying or "distributing" fund is a fund certified by the Board of Inland Revenue as one which pursues a full distribution policy (ie. one which is not rolling up and has never rolled up its income).

An offshore income gain is calculated as if it were a capital gain but without regard to indexation allowance. Thus the gain is normally the difference between the disposal proceeds and original cost. The offshore income gain is deducted from the disposal consideration when calculating the gain for CGT purposes.

Example

Adrian sells 500 units in the Albione Unit Trust, a non-qualifying offshore fund, on 14 May 1996 for £5,000, having purchased them on 12 June 1987 for £3,200.

Adrian's offshore income gain is:	£
Sale proceeds	5,000
Less: cost	(3,200)
Schedule D Case VI assessment	£1,800

Adrian's CGT position is:	£
Sale proceeds	5,000
Reduced by offshore income gain	(1,800)
	3,200
Less: cost	(3,200)
Gain	nil

5.5 Tax Exempt Special Savings Accounts (TESSAs)

Any individual aged 18 or over may have one TESSA, at a bank or a building society. TESSAs are ordinary interest-bearing savings accounts, but so long as the conditions are met all interest is tax-free. Any bonus paid on the account is also disregarded for capital gains tax purposes.

ss.326A - C;
s.271(4) TCGA
1992

Up to £3,000 may be invested in the first 12 months from the opening of the account, then up to £1,800 per 12 month period thereafter. The total invested must not exceed £9,000.

Withdrawals may be made, but not so as to reduce the remaining balance below the sum of:

(a)   all sums invested; and

(b)   any interest so far credited x the appropriate rate of tax when it was credited.

The appropriate rate is the basic rate (25%) for interest credited up to 5 April 1996 and the lower rate (20%) thereafter.

If a withdrawal breaking this condition is made, all interest credited to date becomes taxable in the year of the withdrawal.

After five years, the account ceases to be a TESSA and the whole balance may be withdrawn. The taxpayer may then open another TESSA and start again from scratch.

Alternatively, the taxpayer can reinvest the *capital* from a matured account into a 'follow-up' TESSA. The amount of the capital reinvested must exceed £3,000. The maximum is £9,000. No further amounts may be invested in the first year, but thereafter a maximum of £1,800 can be invested each year until the £9,000 maximum capital deposit is reached.

s.326BB

The reinvestment must take place within 6 months of the old account maturing, and the new account must be held for 5 years to qualify for relief.

If the taxpayer dies, the balance in the TESSA is paid into his estate and there is no income tax liability.

TESSAs may be transferable from one bank or building society to another such body which operates TESSAs depending on the terms of the account.

5.6   Personal Equity Plans (PEPs)

5.6.1   Introduction

Under the personal equity plan (PEP) scheme, any individual, aged 18 or over, who is resident and ordinarily resident in the UK, can invest up to £6,000 (by lump sum or instalments) per tax year in a PEP.

s.333; SI 1989/469

An individual may invest in only one ordinary PEP per year, regardless of the amount invested. However, an individual may also invest up to £3,000 a year in a 'corporate PEP' or 'single company PEP' which invests only in the shares of one company.

5.6.2   Tax reliefs

Provided a PEP meets all the necessary conditions, the investor is entitled to the following reliefs on gains and income arising from a PEP.

(a)   All capital gains on disposals are free of tax

(b)   All withdrawals of capital are free of capital gains tax

(c)   All dividends and interest payments are exempt from income tax. The associated tax credits (at 20% on grossed up dividends and interest) are reclaimed from the Revenue by the plan manager

However disposals of PEP assets at a loss do not give rise to allowable losses for capital gains tax purposes.

PEPs are most advantageous to those who pay higher rate income tax and fully use their annual capital gains tax exemption (currently £6,300). However, in the long term PEPs may benefit others in that they may be used to build up substantial tax exempt funds.

5.6.3   Qualifying investments

Funds invested in a PEP must be applied in acquiring qualifying investments. These are:

(a)   ordinary shares (except of investment trusts) of companies that are:

    (i)   incorporated in the European Union (EU); and

    (ii)   listed on the UK stock exchange, quoted on the USM or listed on a recognised stock exchange in any member state of the EU

(b)   specified corporate bonds of UK non-financial companies, which carry a fixed rate of interest and have a term of at least 5 years to maturity

(c)   preference shares in UK and EU companies

(d)   units in authorised unit trusts and shares in investment trusts, up to the full £6,000 a year. Such investments may not be made in corporate PEPs

(e)   cash. Interest earned is tax-free so long as the interest is eventually invested in shares or in unit or investment trusts. Any interest not so invested is taxable in full on being paid to the investor, and must be paid to him net of lower rate tax if the total interest so paid in a year exceeds £180. In a corporate PEP, any cash invested or obtained from a sale of shares must be used to buy shares within six weeks

Paired shares, comprising UK and foreign shares which can only be sold as a pair, are treated as if they were units in a unit trust.

Unit and investment trusts invested in must themselves invest at least 50% of their funds in ordinary shares which would qualify under the rules set out in (a) above or in investment trusts or unit trusts which themselves so invest (but a unit trust investing in unit trusts must invest all of its funds in such unit trusts). However, a PEP may invest up to a quarter of the subscription limit (£6,000/4 = £1,500) a year (plus re-invested income) in authorised unit trusts and investment trusts which invest at least 50% of their funds in listed ordinary shares which need not qualify under the rules set out in (a) above (for example listed shares in American companies). Such investments must not take the total value of such investments above 25% of the total value of the portfolio (but securities need not be sold merely because market values alter).

Where a taxpayer acquires newly-issued shares qualifying under the rules set out in (a) above in a public offer, he may transfer them directly into the PEP within six weeks from allocation of the shares.

Shares acquired under an approved profit sharing scheme or an approved savings related share option scheme may (subject to the £3,000 a year limit, valuing the shares at market value) be transferred directly to a corporate PEP within six weeks of emerging from the scheme, with no capital gains tax charge on the transfer to the PEP. Shares in unquoted, non-European Union or investment trust companies may enter corporate PEPs by this route, but not by purchase in the open market except where dividends from transferred shares are re-invested.

5.7   The Enterprise Investment Scheme (EIS)

5.7.1   Introduction

The EIS is intended to encourage investment in the ordinary shares of unquoted companies. When a qualifying individual subscribes for eligible shares in a qualifying company, the amount subscribed (including any share premium) is a tax reducer, saving tax at 20%. Relief must be claimed within 12 months of the Inland Revenue's authorising the company to issue a certificate to the investor that the share issue qualifies for relief.

s289

s.289A

5.7.2   The conditions for relief

A *qualifying individual* is one who is not connected with the company at any time in the period from two years before the issue (or from incorporation if later) to five years after the issue. An individual is connected with the company in any of the following circumstances.

ss.191 - 191B

(a)   He (either alone or with his associates) possesses or is entitled to acquire more than 30% of the ordinary shares, the share capital plus loan capital or the voting power in the company or any subsidiary

(b)   On a winding up of the company or any subsidiary, he (either alone or with his associates) would be entitled to more than 30% of the assets

(c)   He (either alone or with his associates) controls the company or any subsidiary

(d)   He is a partner of the company or of any subsidiary

(e)   He is an employee or a non-qualifying director of the company or of a subsidiary, or of a partner of the company or of a subsidiary. A qualifying director who is also an employee is not treated as connected under this rule

Associates include partners, spouses, parents or remoter forebears and children or remoter issue.

A *qualifying director* is one who does not receive payment from the company apart from the following amounts.

s.291A

(a)   Reasonable remuneration for his services (as director or employee). However, even reasonable remuneration will make a director non-qualifying unless, either on the current share issue or on some other issue within the previous five years, the director subscribed for shares eligible for EIS relief at a time when he had never been connected with the company and had never been employed by someone carrying on the company's trade

(b)   Reimbursements of expenses

(c)   Reasonable interest on loans and dividends giving a normal return on shares

(d)   Reasonable payment for goods and reasonable rent for property

(e)   Reasonable remuneration for non-managerial services provided in the course of the director's trade or profession (for example as a solicitor or a plumber)

Eligible shares are newly issued ordinary shares which carry no preferential rights to dividends, assets or redemption in the five years from the date of issue.

A *qualifying company is* a company which satisfies all of the following conditions throughout the three years from the issue of the shares (or from the start of trade if later).

s.293

(a)   Its shares are not marketed to the general public. They are so marketed if they are listed on the Stock Exchange, quoted on the Unlisted Securities Market or quoted on specified overseas markets

(b)   It exists wholly to carry on one or more qualifying trades, to carry out research and development intended to lead to such a trade or to hold shares and securities in companies carrying out qualifying trades or research and development

(c)   At any time in the three year period when the trade or the research and development is being carried on, it is carried on wholly or mainly in the UK

(d)   All of its issued shares are fully paid up

(e)   It does not control, either alone or with connected persons, any other company (except for 90% subsidiaries which carry on qualifying trades or research and development, hold and manage property for the group's qualifying activities, or are dormant) and it is not under the control of another company (whether alone or with connected persons)

A *qualifying trade* is one carried on commercially with a view to profit. The following activities are excluded.

s.297

(a)   Dealing in goods other than in an ordinary trade of wholesale or retail distribution

(b)   Investing in goods of a kind which are normally collected or held as investments, for example fine wines, if the stock is not sold at the rate one would expect in a trading concern

(c)   Dealing in commodities, futures, shares, securities, other financial instruments or land

(d)   Financial activities such as banking, hire purchase and insurance

(e)   The provision of legal and accountancy services

(f)   Oil extraction activities (but exploration for oil in the UK is permitted)

(g)   Leasing, apart from chartering of ships (other than oil rigs and pleasure craft) for up to 12 months at a time

(h)   The receipt of royalties or licence fees, except in respect of a company's research and development or by a film production company

5.7.3 Limits on relief

There is a monetary limit on the amount of qualifying share capital that a company can raise (in one issue or a series of issues) in the longer of:

s.290A

(a)   six months ending on the date of the issue; or

(b)   the period from the start of the tax year to the date of the issue.

The monetary limit is £1,000,000, but it is £5,000,000 where the company's trade is ship chartering.

Where a company (or any of its subsidiaries) carries on a trade in partnership or as a joint venture, the limit is divided by the number of partners to the venture. The £50,000 limit for companies with substantial land and buildings is divided by the same number.

The maximum total investment that can qualify in a tax year is £100,000 per individual. If an investment is less than £500 no relief is available (unless subscription is made by an approved EIS fund, which pools the contributions of several investors).

s.290

Generally speaking, relief is given on an actual basis: a 1996/97 investment will attract relief against 1996/97 tax. However, a taxpayer can claim to treat up to half of his EIS investments made between 6 April and 5 October in a tax year as made in the previous tax year, subject to a maximum carryback from any one year of £15,000.

If full relief is not obtained in a tax year (because the £100,000 limit is exceeded or the taxpayer has insufficient tax to be reduced), the relief obtained is apportioned between the shares issued in the year in proportion to the amounts subscribed. This will determine how much relief is withdrawn should that happen. If issues are treated as made in the previous year, they are also so treated for the purposes of this rule.

5.7.4 Disposals of shares

If an individual disposes of shares (or receives value from the company, for example by taking a loan from the company, but excluding rights issues at a discount and sales of rights) within five years of their issue, the tax reduction obtained may be wholly or partly withdrawn. The tax reduction is withdrawn by assessing the individual under Schedule D Case VI.

s.299 - 301

If the shares are given away or sold otherwise than at arm's length within the five years, all of the tax reduction is withdrawn.

On an arm's length sale or a receipt of value within the five years, the tax reduction to be withdrawn is:

$$\text{Consideration obtained} \times \frac{\text{Tax reduction obtained on issue}}{\text{Issue price of shares}}$$

However, the withdrawal cannot exceed the tax reduction originally obtained (which may have been less than 20% of the issue price, for example because the individual did not have enough tax to reduce).

When shares of the same class were acquired at different times, shares acquired earlier are deemed to be disposed of before shares acquired later (a first in, first out rule). This rule also applies for CGT purposes, overriding the normal CGT rules. However, bonus shares are treated as acquired at the same time as the shares which gave rise to the entitlement to them.

A transfer of shares between spouses does not give rise to a withdrawal of the tax reduction. The reduction obtained remains associated with the shares, and if the recipient spouse disposes of the shares outside the marriage within five years of their issue, it is withdrawn by an assessment on the recipient spouse.

The death of a shareholder is not treated as a disposal.

If shares are disposed of after five years from issue, the following consequences ensue.

(a)   The tax reduction is not withdrawn (although earlier partial withdrawals stand)

(b)   If there is a gain for CGT purposes it is exempt

s.150A TCGA 1992

(c)   Any loss for CGT purposes is restricted by reducing the issue price (but not so as to create a gain). The reduction is the tax reduction obtained and not withdrawn

When shares issued under the EIS are sold at arm's length at a loss at any time (within or outside the first five years), and the EIS relief is not wholly withdrawn, the loss may be relieved against income under s 574 ICTA 1988. See the Business Taxation text for this relief.

Example

In 1996/97, David subscribes for shares under the EIS. The amount subscribed is £34,000, but because of a shortage of tax to reduce the tax reduction obtained is only £5,000. Half of the shares are sold for £12,000 after three years, and the other half are sold for £25,000 after six years, giving a gain (as computed for CGT purposes) of £3,270. Both sales are at arm's length.

(a) **How much tax reduction must David pay back to the Inland Revenue on the first sale?**

(b) **How much of the gain on the second sale is exempt, and how much is chargeable to CGT?**

Solution

(a) The tax reduction obtained on the shares sold after three years was £5,000/2 = £2,500. The issue price was £34,000/2 = £17,000.

The amount which David must pay back to the Inland Revenue is £12,000 x £2,500/£17,000 = £1,765.

(b) The full gain of £3,270 is exempt.

5.7.5 Replacement capital

The EIS is not meant to be used to obtain a tax reduction for capital which is essentially replacing other capital invested by the same individuals. A tax reduction obtained is therefore withdrawn if, at any time from two years before to five years after the later of the issue of shares and the commencement of trade, the company takes over a trade which is more than half owned by the individual or by a group of persons including him, or which is carried on by a company controlled by him or by a group of persons including him. However, where a trade is taken over from a company, the tax reduction is only withdrawn if the individual or the group of persons including him also controls the company which issued the EIS shares.

s.302

5.8   Venture Capital Trusts (VCTs)

5.8.1   Tax reducer on investment

With effect from 6 April 1995 an individual who is at least 18 years of age who subscribes for new eligible shares in a Venture Capital Trust (VCT) will usually be entitled to claim income tax relief in respect of his investment. The amount of income tax relief available to such an individual is the lower of:

Sch 15B para 1(1)-(5)

(a)   20% of the amount subscribed for eligible shares in VCTs in the year of assessment up to a maximum of £100,000 per tax year; and

(b)   the individual's income tax liability for the year.

5.8.2   Additional relief from income tax

Relief on Distributions

Dividends (including capital dividends) received by an individual who is at least 18 years of age in respect of ordinary shares in a VCT are exempt from income tax, provided:

(a)   The company was a VCT when the individual acquired his shares; and

(b)   The dividend is paid out of profits, etc. which accrued to the company in an accounting period ending after its approval as a VCT; and

(c)   The shares in respect of which the dividend is paid were not acquired by the investor in excess of the permitted maximum £100,000 investment for any year of assessment

Sch 15B paras 7 & 8

Distribution relief is available to individuals who acquired VCT shares by purchase on the Stock Exchange (or by gift, or in any other manner). It is not necessary for the individual to subscribe for new VCT shares.

The relief on distributions is given on the first £100,000 of ordinary shares acquired in each tax year at a time when the company was a VCT. The 20% relief on investment is given on the first £100,0000 of new VCT ordinary shares subscribed for in each tax year.

Sch 15B para 8

Example

> Miss Davidson acquired existing ordinary shares in VCT1 with a value of £30,000 on 1 May 1996. On 1 December 1996 she subscribed £100,000 for new ordinary shares in VCT2.
>
> 1.   The VCT1 shares will qualify for relief on distributions.
>
> 2.   The £100,000 invested in VCT2 shares will qualify for the 20% relief on investment and £70,000 of the investment will qualify for relief on distributions.

5.8.3   Conditions for relief

VCTs are companies which are approved by the Board of Inland Revenue. The main conditions for approval are that the VCT is not a close company and in its most recent complete accounting period:

s.842AA

(a)   Its ordinary share capital has been quoted throughout the period on the Stock Exchange

(b)   Its income has been derived wholly or mainly from shares or securities

(c)   At least 70% by value of its investments has been represented throughout the period by shares or securities (including loans of at least five years' duration) in qualifying holdings. Qualifying holdings are (broadly) holdings in unquoted companies carrying on qualifying trades in the UK. The value of an investment is normally taken to be its value when acquired, but where it is added to at a later date it is its value immediately after the addition

(d)   At least 50% of its qualifying holdings throughout the period has been represented by eligible shares

(e)   No holding in any company – other than in another VCT or a company which would qualify as a VCT if it were quoted – has at any time in the period represented more than 15% by value of its total investments

(f)   It has not retained more than 15% of the income it derived from shares and securities; ie. it must distribute an amount equal to 85% of its income from shares and securities and 100% of any other income. However, this distribution requirement is waived if the amount required to satisfy the 15% rule is less than £10,000 per 12 month accounting period

The above conditions must also be satisfied during the company's current accounting period.

The Revenue will specify the date from which a VCT is approved. This cannot be earlier than the date on which application for approval was made by the company.

Approval may be withdrawn where a VCT ceases to satisfy the above conditions or fails to satisfy such conditions within the above time periods. A notice of withdrawal of approval normally has effect from the time it is given.

Qualifying Holdings

For a holding in a "relevant company" to be a qualifying holding: Sch 28B

(a)   The relevant company must have issued the shares or securities to the VCT and they must have been held by the VCT ever since; ie. there must be a new issue of shares. Shares, etc. purchased from an existing shareholder cannot be qualifying holdings

(b)   The relevant company must be unquoted and its shares must not be dealt in on the USM. However, where such a company later becomes quoted it is deemed to remain unquoted for a period of five years after it first ceased to be so   Sch 28B para 2

(c)   The relevant company (and any qualifying subsidiaries) must carry on a qualifying trade wholly or mainly in the UK, or must be preparing to carry on such a trade and commence it within two years after the date of issue of shares, etc. to the VCT

(d)   The money received by the relevant company from the issue of shares, etc. to the VCT must be used wholly for the purposes of its qualifying trade within (normally) 12 months from the time the relevant holding was issued   Sch 28B para 6

(e)   The amount invested by the VCT in the relevant company must not exceed £1 million in any six month period or in any year of assessment   Sch 28B para 7

(f)   The value of the relevant company's assets as a whole must not exceed £10 million immediately before the relevant holding is issued to the VCT   Sch 28B para 8

(g)   The relevant company must not be controlled by another company and if it has any subsidiary companies they must all be 90% qualifying subsidiaries   Sch 28B paras 9 & 10

(h)   At least 50% by value of a VCT's qualifying holdings must be represented by eligible shares. Eligible shares are ordinary shares with no present or future preferential rights to dividends, assets in a winding up, or redemption

s.842AA(14)

Qualifying Trades

Sch 28B paras 3-5

All trades (including research and development from which it is intended that a trade will be derived) are qualifying trades except for certain prohibited activities:

(a)   Dealing in land, in commodities or futures or in shares, securities or other financial instruments

(b)   Dealing in goods, otherwise than in the course of an ordinary trade of wholesale or retail distribution

(c)   Banking, insurance, money-lending, debt-factoring, hire-purchase financing or other financial activities

(d)   Leasing (including letting ships on charter or other assets on hire) or receiving royalties or licence fees

(e)   Providing legal or accountancy services

(f)   Providing services or facilities for any such trade carried on by another person if it:

    (i)   consists, to a substantial extent, in activities within any of paragraphs (a) to (e) above; and

    (ii)   is a trade in which a controlling interest is held by a person who also has a controlling interest in the trade carried on by the company providing the services or facilities.

Sch 28B para 4

Note that building and construction, property development for resale and farming are not prohibited activities of the relevant company, and there is no restriction on the amount to the relevant company's assets that can be in the form of land and buildings.

5.8.4   Withdrawal of relief

VCT income tax investment relief is withdrawn if the investor disposes of his shares in the VCT within five years of their issue. A disposal at a profit or other than by way of a bargain at arm's length results in a withdrawal of the full relief. A disposal by bargain at arm's length for less than the cost of the shares results in a clawback of relief equal to the consideration received multiplied by the lower rate of income tax for the tax year in which the relief was given. The death of the investor or a disposal to a spouse does not result in any withdrawal of relief.

VCT income tax relief is also withdrawn if the VCT loses it approved status within five years after issuing eligible shares to the investor. In such circumstances the investor's full income tax relief is withdrawn.

Sch 15B para 3

Withdrawals of VCT income tax investment relief are made by way of Schedule D Case VI assessments for the year of assessment for which the relief was originally given.

Sch 15B para 4

Investors are required to give notice to their Inspector of Taxes within 60 days if an event occurs which gives rise to withdrawal of relief. Similarly, an Inspector may serve a notice requiring such information where he has reason to believe that an individual has not given notice.

Sch 15B para 5

5.9 Pensions

5.9.1 Introduction

The main ways in which individuals can provide for a pension are:

(a)   the state pension scheme;

(b)   occupational pension schemes;

(c)   personal pension schemes;

(d)   retirement annuity schemes.

The state scheme has no impact on income tax during an individual's working career, but the other three systems are discussed below.

5.9.2 Occupational pensions

An employer may set up a pension scheme for employees. Such a scheme may either require contributions from employees or be non-contributory. The employer may use the services of an insurance company (an insured scheme) or may set up a totally self administered pension fund.

s.590

Schemes can be of two kinds: Revenue approved and unapproved. Approved schemes have significant tax advantages that have made them very popular.

The Revenue may withdraw approval of a scheme if approval is no longer warranted, or if the scheme is changed in a way which has not been approved, either specifically or through being on the list of changes which do not require individual approval.

If a scheme is Revenue approved:

s.592

(a)   Contributions made by the employee are deductible from his Schedule E income (up to a limit of 15% of gross emoluments, with gross emoluments limited to the earnings cap (see below))

(b)   The employer's contributions actually paid (not merely provided for) are deductible in calculating profits subject to tax (although deductions for large contributions above the normal level may be spread over several years)

(c)   The employer's contributions are not regarded as benefits in kind for the employee

(d)   The fund of contributions, and the income and gains arising from their investment, are not liable to tax. It is this long-term tax free accumulation of funds that makes approved schemes so beneficial

(e)   Provision can be made for a lump sum to be paid on the employee's death in service. Provided that it does not exceed four times his final remuneration, it is tax-free

(f)   A tax-free lump sum may be paid to the employee on retirement

(g)   The eventual pension is treated as earned income of the retired employee

The following limits apply to an approved occupational pension scheme:

(a)   The maximum pension is normally two thirds of the individual's final remuneration, being calculated as one sixtieth for each year of service, with a maximum of 40 years.

The pension must start at an age between 60 and 75. The pension can be taken flexibly to defer a higher pension for later years to fund the need for increasing care facilities

(b)   A scheme may provide for part of the pension to be taken as a lump sum. The maximum lump sum is 1.5 times final remuneration, being calculated as 3/80 for each year of service, with a maximum of 40 years

The Revenue have discretion to approve schemes which do not comply with these limits. In particular, many schemes provide for a pension of two thirds of final salary after less than 40 years service

The earnings cap

An earnings cap applies to tax-approved occupational pension schemes. The cap is £82,200 for 1996/97.

s.590C

The earnings cap has two consequences.

(a)   The maximum pension payable from an approved scheme is the cap x 2/3

(b)   The maximum tax-free lump sum is the cap x 1.5

The earnings cap does not apply if the scheme was set up before 14 March 1989 *and* the employee joined the scheme before 1 June 1989.

Additional voluntary contributions

An employee who feels that his employer's scheme is inadequate may make additional voluntary contributions (AVCs), either to the employer's scheme or to a separate scheme operated by an insurance company (freestanding AVCs). AVCs are deductible from the employee's taxable pay, but only to the extent that they, plus any contributions by the employee to the employer's scheme, do not exceed 15% of gross emoluments (limited to the earnings cap). The limits on pensions and lump sums which may be taken must be applied to the total sums derived from the employer's scheme and the AVCs.

Sch 23, para 7;
SI 1987/1749

Freestanding AVCs are paid net of basic rate tax.

Employers are permitted to establish unapproved schemes, to operate alongside approved schemes. But an employer's contributions to an unapproved pension scheme will be taxed as the earnings of the employee and the employee's contributions will not be tax-deductible.

All employees, including owner-directors of small companies, may join approved schemes. The creation of a self-administered pension scheme is an important part of tax planning for the smaller company. However, regulations restrict the extent to which pension schemes can invest in the companies setting them up (a common practice with smaller companies).

5.9.3   Personal pension schemes

Personal pension schemes (PPSs) are a means of providing pensions to the self-employed and to those in non-pensionable employment (which includes employees who choose not to join their employer's occupational scheme; employees cannot be forced to join such a scheme).

The taxpayer makes a contract with a life assurance company or other pension provider and pays premiums. An individual's employer may also contribute. Such a contribution is not a taxable emolument in the hands of the employee, to the extent that the employer's contribution is within the appropriate limit on premiums, for example 17$\frac{1}{2}$% of earnings (see below). The premiums go into a fund which is invested and is ultimately used to provide a pension.

s.632

s.643

The taxpayer may also use his PPS to contract out of the State earnings related pension scheme (SERPS). If he does so, the Department of Social Security pays premiums into his scheme, in addition to his own premiums and without reducing the maximum premiums he can pay. He must still pay full (not contracted out) national insurance contributions.

Tax reliefs

(a)   The taxpayer may deduct his premium from his earnings, up to a percentage of 'net relevant earnings' that depends on his age. Employees (but not the self-employed) pay PPS contributions net of basic rate tax. The allowable premium should be shown as a deduction from the source of income to which it relates in the individual's personal tax computation. If a premium is paid net of basic rate tax, that tax must be added to tax borne in arriving at tax payable, just like the tax on charges paid net

s.639

(b)   The pensions part of the life assurance company's business is tax exempt, so both capital gains on and income from investments bought with premiums are tax free

(c)   The pension on retirement is treated as earned income of the taxpayer

Eligibility

To be eligible to take out a PPS the taxpayer must have relevant earnings. That is either he is self-employed or he has emoluments taxable under Schedule E which do not provide rights in an occupational pension scheme.

It is also possible for an individual in pensionable employment to have a PPS, provided that his scheme does not permit contributions from the employee or the employer. Thus the DSS contributions for someone contracting out of SERPS may be paid into a personal pension scheme.

Limits on contributions

The deductible percentages of net relevant earnings are shown on page (viii).

Net relevant earnings (NRE) is calculated thus.

s.646

		£	£
Earnings under Schedule D Cases I and II			X
Schedule E emoluments not providing pension scheme rights			X
Schedule A income from furnished holiday lettings			X
			X
Less:	the excess of trade charges over other income	X	
	capital allowances	X	
	loss relief*	X	
	Schedule E deductions	X	
			(X)
Net relevant earnings			X

*   Relief for a trading loss can be taken against STI which would include any non-trading income of the taxpayer. Where a trading loss has relieved non-trading income it remains intact for reducing net relevant earnings for the next tax year and any further tax year if necessary.

Example

Ross has the following trading results:

Year ended 31 December 1993	£10,000
Year ended 31 December 1994	(5,000)
Year ended 31 December 1995	12,000
Year ended 31 December 1996	18,000

The loss of £5,000 is claimed against other income under s.380(1) ICTA 1988 (see Business Income Tax and VAT text, Session 6) in 1994/95.

Solution

Ross has NRE of £10,000 for 1994/95; nil for 1995/96; and only £10,000 (15,000* - 5,000) for 1996/97 since the loss claim against other income is not recognised for NRE purposes.

*The 1996/97 assessment under the Schedule D I transitional rules is 50% of the profits for the two years ending in 1996/97.

Non-trading charges (for example under a deed of covenant) are not deducted in arriving at NRE even if there is insufficient other income to deduct them from.

Some of the premium paid can be used to secure a lump sum or an annuity for a spouse or dependants in the event of death prior to retirement age. The limit (which forms part of the overall limit) for such premiums is 5% of NRE.

Net relevant earnings are restricted to the same earnings cap as applies for occupational schemes (£82,200 for 1996/97).

s.640A

The maximum tax deductible premium payable by an employee is restricted if the employer also contributes. The employee's tax deductible limit is the limit that would apply for his age less the employer's contribution.

Relating back premiums

Relief for a premium is given primarily against NRE of the tax year in which the premium is actually paid. An election may, however, be made for any premium to be treated as if paid in the previous tax year or, if NRE was nil in that previous year, as if paid in the year before that (related back two years). This election is valuable to an individual whose income for the previous period was higher (and possibly taxed at a higher rate). The taxpayer can relate back any specified part of a premium.

The time limit for the election is for 1996/97 onwards is 31 January following the end of the tax year in which the premium was actually paid.

s.641

Unused relief

Unused relief is the amount by which premiums paid are less than the maximum calculated as a percentage of NRE. It can be carried forward for six years. For example, in 1996/97 unused relief from 1990/91 (six years earlier) to 1995/96 could be taken into account to increase the maximum allowable premium.

s.642

The relief available for a particular tax year must be used *before* unused relief brought forward, and the oldest relief brought forward is used first (a first in, first out basis).

Any contributions in excess of the amount eligible for relief must be repaid to the taxpayer.

Example

An individual born in 1967 who took out a PPS on 1 July 1993 has the following NRE and paid the following gross premiums.

	NRE	$17\frac{1}{2}\%$ of NRE	Gross premiums
	£	£	£
1993/94	35,000	6,125	5,800
1994/95	33,000	5,775	5,700
1995/96	38,000	6,650	6,850
1996/97	43,000	7,525	8,000

Show the relief available for premiums paid.

Solution

1993/94	£
$17\frac{1}{2}\%$ of NRE	6,125
Less: premium paid	(5,800)
Unused relief	£325

1994/95	£
$17\frac{1}{2}\%$ of NRE	5,775
Less: premium paid	(5,700)
Unused relief	£75

1995/96	£
$17\frac{1}{2}\%$ of NRE	6,650
Unused relief 1993/94 (part)	200
	6,850
Less: premium paid	(6,850)
Unused relief	nil

1996/97	£
$17\frac{1}{2}\%$ of NRE	7,525
Unused relief: 1993/94 (balance)	125
1994/95	75
	7,725
Less: premium paid	(8,000)
Unrelieved premium (must be repaid)	£275

Benefits on retirement

Benefits can be taken under a PPS from the age of 50 (whether or not the recipient actually stops work) and must begin at age 75 at the latest. For certain occupations (such as a dancer or a cricketer) and in cases of ill health the Revenue may allow benefits to be taken earlier.

s.634

The taxpayer must receive his pension in the form of an annuity bought with the savings built up in the scheme. This annuity is normally purchased from the same pension provider that has managed the fund before retirement, but some pension plans allow the taxpayer to buy his annuity elsewhere. Part of the funds may, however, be used to produce a lump sum tax free cash payment. The maximum lump sum allowed is 25% of the value of the fund.

ss.634, 635

The annuity bought with the part of the fund not taken as a lump sum is paid net of basic rate tax up to 5 April 1995. From 6 April 1995 such annuities will be paid under PAYE so as to take account of the pensioner's allowances.

A purchased life annuity is taxed at the lower rate where the annuitant is not a higher rate tax payer.

It is often sensible to take the maximum lump sum permitted, even if the pensioner would prefer a regular income, as the lump sum can then be used to buy an annuity to last for his life. Part of each annuity payment bought in this way will be treated as a return of capital and will therefore be tax free.

A member of a personal pension scheme can defer the purchase of an annuity until a maximum age of 75 years. During the deferral period a member of a scheme may make income withdrawals from the scheme. Income withdrawals must be between 35% and 100% of the annuity which would have been purchasable by the member. Income withdrawals are assessed under Schedule E.

s.634A

Investments

PPSs may allow the scheme member to direct how his contributions are invested. However, no investments may be acquired from or sold to the scheme member, though the scheme may let commercial property to the scheme member's business on commercial terms.

5.9.4 Retirement annuity schemes

Retirement annuity schemes (RASs) were the predecessor of PPSs. PPSs were introduced on 1 July 1988, and RASs in existence before that date continue in force and remain subject to the rules governing RASs. A taxpayer with an RAS may, if he wishes, also start a PPS.

ss.618 - 629

The RAS rules are as same as the PPS rules, except as follows:

(a)   An individual's employer may not contribute to an RAS

(b)   The earnings cap does not apply: net relevant earnings of any amount may be taken into account

(c)   The limit on premiums as a percentage of net relevant earnings are shown on page (viii)

(d)   Benefits must commence between ages 60 and 75. Benefits may be taken earlier for certain occupations and in cases of ill health

(e)   The maximum lump sum which may be taken on retirement is three times the annuity which can be purchased with the rest of the fund

If a taxpayer wishes to pay premiums under both a RAS and a PPS in the same year of assessment, then:

(a)   the maximum RAS premium is determined under the usual RAS rules ($17^1/2\%$ to $27^1/2\%$ of NRE);

(b)   the maximum PPS premium is:

    (i)   the maximum under the usual PPS rules ($17^1/2\%$ to 40% of NRE); minus

    (ii)   the RAS premium actually paid and for which tax relief has been given.

(c)   the maximum relief available for carry-forward is:

    (i)   RAR: (a) less RAP and PPS paid and relieved

    (ii)   PPS: (b) less PPS paid and relieved.

5.10 Life assurance policies

5.10.1 Qualifying policies

Life assurance policies are often used as a way of saving, rather than to protect dependants on the insured person's early death. Qualifying life assurance policies benefit from a tax exemption on maturity or surrender. Life assurance policies suitable as a means of saving (long-term policies) are not subject to the insurance premium tax which applies to, for example, household and car insurance.

A policy is qualifying if:

Sch 15 Part 1

(a)   It is taken out on the policyholder's or his spouse's life

(b)   The company involved trades in the UK

(c)   The policy secures a capital sum on death, earlier disability, or a date not before the tenth anniversary of taking out the policy

(d)   The premiums are reasonably even and are payable annually or at shorter intervals

(e)   At least a certain capital sum is assured:

    (i)   for endowment policies, 75% of the total premiums payable;

    (ii)   for whole life policies, 75% of the premiums payable up to age 75.

Gifts worth up to £30, such as are commonly offered to induce people to take out policies, do not render policies non-qualifying.

Any profit (the surplus of proceeds over total premiums paid) on maturity or surrender of the policy is free of all tax. However, if the policy is surrendered within a period which is less than ten years and less than 3/4 of the term, any gain on the policy is taxed as if it were non-qualifying (see below).

5.10.2 Non-qualifying policies

Non-qualifying life policies are often advertised as 'investment bonds' or 'property bonds'. They often take the form of a fixed term lump sum investment by a policyholder who also enjoys life cover during the term. The overall gain on the policy may be liable to tax at the excess of the higher rate over the lower rate. Top slicing relief is available to mitigate the tax. However, during the term of the policy any investment gains and income are taxed only in the hands of the insurance company.

s.539

Partial surrenders are allowed without incurring any immediate tax liability. The limit is 5% a year of the premium on a cumulative basis up to a maximum of 100%. Suppose, for example, that an investor purchased a £30,000 single premium bond in 1990. In 1996 he is short of income. He can effect a partial surrender for £9,000 (6 years x 5% x £30,000) without incurring any immediate tax liability.

When the policy is finally encashed, any tax-free withdrawals are added to the amount received on encashment to determine the overall tax liability. There is no basic rate or lower rate liability. In addition, any tax at the higher rate is determined using the *top slicing* rules:

s.550

(a)   Calculate the overall profit from the policy (proceeds on encashment + early withdrawals - initial premium)

(b)   Divide the overall profit by the number of complete years since the policy was taken out

(c)   Calculate the increase in the taxpayer's total tax liability that arises from adding the slice found in (b) to his other sources of income. The slice is added above all other income, *including dividends and termination payments*. Remember that the slice is only liable to tax at the higher rate

(d)   Multiply the increase found in (c) by the number of years used in (b) to find the amount of tax payable

If, before final encashment, withdrawals exceed the permitted limit, the excess is taxable immediately at the higher rate. Again, top slicing applies. The slice is found by dividing the excess by the number of years since the policy was taken out (or, if appropriate, since the last excess occurred). In calculating the tax on final encashment, the excess(es) are excluded from the calculation of the overall profit since they have been taxed already.

Example

An investor took out a single premium policy on 31 October 1990 for £15,000. He withdrew 4% of the premium in each of the next five years and he encashed the policy on 30 June 1996 receiving £20,000. In the tax year 1996/97 his other income (all Schedule E) was £24,200 after deducting his personal allowance.

Calculate the amount of tax payable in respect of the bond.

Solution

	£
Proceeds	20,000
Withdrawals 5 x £600	3,000
	23,000
Less: initial premium	(15,000)
Profit	£8,000

Number of complete years = 5
One slice = £8,000/5 = £1,600
Tax liabilities are as follows:

	Without slice £	With slice £
Other income after personal allowance	24,200	24,200
Slice	nil	1,600
Taxable income	£24,200	£25,800
Tax: at 20% on £3,900	780	780
at 24% on £20,300	4,872	4,872
at 24% on £1,300 (balance)		312
at 40% on £300		120
	5,652	6,084
Less: basic rate tax on slice		
£1,600 x 24%	n/a	(384)
		5,700
	£5,652	(5,652)
Extra tax due to slice		£48
Tax payable on bond 5 x £48		£240

QUESTIONS

1. The first £70 interest paid on a NSB ..... account in any tax year is exempt from income tax. What sort of account?

2. Schedule D Case VI income is assessed on a preceding year basis, with special rules for opening and closing years. TRUE/FALSE?

3. The accrued income scheme is designed to prevent any tax advantage arising from "bondwashing". What is bondwashing and how (very briefly) does the accrued income scheme counteract it?

4. What is the maximum investment in a TESSA during the calendar year 1996 if it was opened on 1 January 1996, assuming this is the first TESSA for this particular individual?

5. Mr and Mrs Daniels have two sons, Jason aged 16 and Paul aged 19. Who in the Daniels family may invest in PEPs?

6. Which of the following individuals may not obtain EIS relief on the cost of subscribing for shares in a qualifying company?

    (a) an individual who, together with his associates, controls 26% of the shares and voting power in the company;

    (b) an unpaid (non-executive) director of the company;

    (c) the managing director's secretary.

7. In the case where an employer sets up a Revenue - approved pension scheme, up to ...% of the employee's emoluments may be contributed to the scheme and qualify for tax relief.

    What percentage?

8. Robin was born on 30 April 1945. He has net relevant earnings for 1996/97 of £16,500. Compute the maximum allowable personal pension scheme contribution for 1996/97, assuming there is no unused relief in prior years.

SOLUTIONS

1.   An ordinary account (5.1.1).

2.   FALSE - Schedule D Case VI income is assessed on an *actual* basis. (5.2).

3.   Bondwashing involves the "conversion" of income into capital, usually by selling fixed interest securities cum interest, shortly before the ex-interest date. The accrued income scheme counteracts this by treating the interest accrued up to the date of transfer as income, rather than as part of the (capital) proceeds on sale of the security. (5.4.1).

4.   £3,000 with a maximum of £1,800 for each succeeding 12 month period. The total investment is limited to £9,000. (5.5)

5.   All of them except Jason, because he is aged under 18. (5.6.1)

6.   (c) - employees are not entitled to relief. (5.7.2)

7.   15% (5.9.2).

8.   £4,125 maximum: £16,500 x 25% (Robin is aged 50 on 6 April 1996). (5.9.3)

SESSION 6

TAXATION OF EMPLOYMENT IN THE UK

The purpose of this session is to:

- explain the scope of the charge to income tax under Schedule E

- describe the rules which assess certain benefits in kind on all employees

- describe the benefit in kind rules relating only to employees paid £8,500 or more p.a. and directors

- provide a summary of benefits which are tax-free for all employees

- explain the statute and case law governing the deductibility of expenses from Schedule E income

- describe the special provisions taxing payments on termination of employment

References: ICTA 1988 unless otherwise stated.

6.1   Basis of the Schedule E charge

6.1.1   Assessable income

'Emoluments' from an office or employment are taxed under Schedule E. The term 'emoluments' includes 'all salaries, fees, wages, perquisites and profits whatsoever'. In particular, liability to Schedule E income tax is not limited to monetary payments; it also includes benefits which are convertible into money (and for employees paid £8,500 or more and directors, benefits which are *not* convertible too).

s.19(1)
s.131(1)

Thus, besides taxing salaries and wages from employment, Schedule E income tax is also charged in respect of:

(a)   various benefits in kind and payments of expenses (see sections 6.2 and 6.3);

(b)   pensions and annuities paid in the UK, whether provided by the State, an occupational pension scheme or a personal pension plan;

(c)   payments made on termination of employment;

(d)   gains realised by a director or employee on exercising, assigning or releasing an option to acquire shares in his employing company; and

s.135(1)

(e)   various social security benefits, notably unemployment benefit.

Note that foreign pensions are assessable under Case V of Schedule D, rather than Schedule E.

Losses cannot arise under Schedule E.

6.1.2　The receipts basis

Emoluments under Schedule E are assessed as income for the year in which they are received. The date of receipt is the earliest of:

ss.202A & 202B

(a)　the date of payment (or payment on account); or

(b)　the date when a person becomes entitled to the payment; or

(c)　in the case of directors only, the earliest of:

　　(i)　the date the emoluments are credited in the company's records or accounts; or

　　(ii)　the end of a period of account if emoluments for that period are determined before the period ends; or

　　(iii)　the date emoluments are determined if the amount is not determined until after the period ends.

Example

A director of a company is entitled under his employment contract to a salary of £24,000 pa. payable monthly on the 24th of each month in equal amounts. Additionally he is entitled to a performance-related bonus calculated on each half year's profits. The company prepares accounts to 31 December each year. His bonus for the six months to 30 June 1996 of £8,000 is determined on 1 November 1996, credited to his account on 1 January 1997 and paid to him with his January salary. His bonus of £11,500 for the six months to 31 December 1996 is not determined until agreed by the shareholders at the AGM on 30 April 1997. It is then entered into the company's records and paid with his May salary.

You are required to calculate his emoluments for 1996/97 and 1997/98.

Solution

1996/97

Basic salary paid 24 April 1996 to 24 March 1997 inclusive	£24,000
Bonus for six months to 30 June 1996 - determined before the end of the period of account - 'received' 31.12.96	£8,000
1997/98 Basic salary (24.4.97 - 24.3.98 inclusive)	£24,000
Bonus for six months to 31 December 1996 - not determined until the AGM and payable etc. subsequently , therefore 'received' 30 April 1997	£11,500

Emoluments are regarded as being credited in the company's accounts even if the director cannot immediately draw the money because of a legal fetter or if the account credited is not in the director's name. However if the amount credited represents an amount to which the director will only be entitled if certain conditions are met, it will not be "received" until the conditions are met. Note that a "fetter" merely delays payment of an amount to which the director is entitled whereas a "condition" is something which must be satisfied before there is a right to remuneration.

IRPR 28.7.89

If a general provision is made for directors' bonuses in preparing the accounts for an AGM this would not normally represent the crediting of remuneration. Instead the amounts determined at the AGM would be "received" as at that date. However where the directors are also the controlling shareholders the Revenue consider that the amounts involved are received when they meet to agree final remuneration after the year end but before the AGM.

Example

Norman, Peter, and Madeline are directors of a company which runs a chain of fashion boutiques and which prepares accounts to 31 December. They each own one third of the share capital. For the year to 31 December 1996 they set their directors' bonuses of £8,200 each at a directors meeting on 1 April 1997 in advance of the AGM held on 1 May 1997.

You are required to state in which tax year the bonuses are assessable.

Solution

As the directors control the company the amounts of £8,200 each are determined on 1 April 1997 and are therefore assessable in 1996/97.

Sometimes remuneration is received after the employee has ceased to work for that employer. This does not affect the tax position of the employee. Emoluments received are taxable, regardless of whether the office or employment is still held at the date of receipt.

s.202A(2)(b)

Pensions and those social security benefits and income support which are taxable are not assessed on the receipts basis but on the basis of the amount accruing in the tax year.

6.1.3 Employment and self-employment

The distinction between *employment* (Schedule E) and *self-employment* (Schedule D) is a fine one. Employment is a contract of *service*, whereas self-employment is a contract *for services*.

The question of whether a person is employed under a contract of service, or performs services under a contract for services and is thereby self-employed, often has to be decided in practice and is a favourite examination topic.

It used to be thought that the deciding factor was the degree of control exercised by one party over the other. The most that can be said now, however, is that control will always have to be considered, although it can no longer be regarded as the sole determining factor; other factors which may be of importance are such matters as:

* whether the person performing the services provides his own equipment;

* whether he hires his own helpers;

* what degree of financial risk he takes;

* what degree of responsibility for investment and management he has; and

* whether and how far he has an opportunity of profiting from sound management in the performance of his task.

In other words, the fundamental test to be applied is whether the person performing the services is performing them as a person *in business on his own account.*

Market Investigations Ltd v Minister for Social Security (1969)

Mr Lorimer was a vision mixer (ie. his job was to determine what the viewer ultimately saw on the TV screen). Vision mixing normally takes place in a studio, owned or hired by the production company, using expensive equipment. Mr Lorimer was employed full time as a vision mixer until January 1985. Thereafter, he left to become freelance.

Hall v Lorimer (1994) STC 23

As a freelance vision mixer, Mr Lorimer had no full time or long term contract with any one company. Bookings were usually for one or two days at a time. Mr Lorimer carried out all work at the studio, using equipment supplied by the studio company. He did not contribute any money to the production of the programme, nor did he share in the profits or losses. He did not hire any staff. He was registered for VAT, paid RAP contributions and had an insurance policy against sickness.

The Court of Appeal held that Mr Lorimer was self employed and highlighted the following points:

- Mr Lorimer ran the risk of bad debts and this is not normally associated with being an employee

- The expenses incurred by Mr Lorimer were different in nature and scale than the likely expenses of an employee

- Mr Lorimer worked for twenty or more companies between 1985 and 1989 and his engagements usually lasted only a day

The Court of Appeal commented that in deciding the issue of employed or self employed, there is no complete exhaustive list of relevant points to be considered. Also, it is a matter of evaluating the overall effect of the detail (rather than looking at the detail itself).

Further guidance as to whether a person is employed or self-employed is provided in a Revenue booklet entitled "Employed or Self-Employed":

IR 56

"If you can answer 'yes' to the following questions, you are probably an *employee*:

Do you have to do the work that you have agreed to undertake yourself (that is, you are not allowed to send a substitute or hire other people to do it)?

Can someone tell you what to do, and when and how to do it?

Does someone provide you with holiday time, sick pay or a pension? (Though a lot of employees don't get any of these.)

Are you paid so much an hour, a week or a given number of hours a week or month?

Do you work wholly or mainly for one business? (But remember that many employees work for more than one employer.)

Are you expected to work at the premises of the person you are working for, or at a place or places they decide? (But remember that a self-employed person, such as a plumber, may by the nature of the job have to work at the premises of the person who engages him.)

If you can answer 'yes' to the following questions, it will usually mean that you are *self-employed*:

Are you ultimately responsible for how the business is run? Do you risk your own capital in the business? Are you responsible for bearing losses as well as taking profits? Do you yourself control what you do, whether you do it, how you do it, when and where you do it? (Though many employees have considerable independence.)

Do you provide the major items of equipment you need to do your job (not just the small tools which many employees provide for themselves)?

Are you free to hire other people, on terms of your own choice, to do the work that you have agreed to undertake? (But remember that an employee may also be authorised to delegate work or to engage others on behalf of his employer.)

Do you have to correct unsatisfactory work in your own time and at your own expense?"

6.2   Benefits in kind assessable on all employees

6.2.1   The general rule

The general rule for benefits received by a lower-paid employee (ie. paid less than £8,500 pa.) is that they can be assessed only in so far as they can be turned into money: ie. the amount that the benefit would fetch if the employee were to dispose of it to a third party (this is often known as the benefit's 'second-hand value'). This principle was established by very early tax cases, notably *Tennant v Smith* in 1893 where it was found that an employee could not be taxed on the benefit of accommodation provided to him because he could not turn this into money. The legislation now provides special rules in a number of specific instances dealt with below.

6.2.2   Vouchers

If an employee receives:

(a)   non-cash vouchers or credit tokens; or   ss.141-144

(b)   exchangeable (eg. gift) vouchers;

he will be assessable on the *cost to the employer of providing* the benefit. In other words, the general rule - that the assessable value of the benefit is its second-hand value - does not apply in this particular case.

If an employee receives a cash voucher, he will be assessable on the sum of money for which the voucher is capable of being exchanged. He is assessed in the year he receives the voucher and is usually taxed under the PAYE system.

It should be noted that luncheon vouchers are tax free if the cost of providing   ESC A2
them does not exceed 15p per working day. Any excess of cost over 15p is taxable.

Entertainment received by employees from third parties, including hospitality   s.155(7)
such as seats at sporting and cultural events, is not normally a taxable benefit. For
employees paid £8,500+ and directors (see definition in paragraph 6.3.1 below)
such a benefit is removed from the scope of the general charge. For all employees,
however, entertainment, hospitality and vouchers and credit tokens for their   s.141(6B)
provision are exempt if: s.142(3B)

(a)   neither the employer nor a person connected with the employer *provides*
        the entertainment; and

(b)   neither the employer nor a person connected with the employer *procured*
        the entertainment (directly or indirectly); and

(c)   the entertainment is provided neither in recognition nor in anticipation of
        particular services which have been or are to be performed.

'Connected' for this purpose has a wide definition but would not extend to normal   s.839
trade customers or suppliers. So the hospitality received by a buyer from his
employer's suppliers would not give rise to a benefit on him.

A car parking space at or near an employee's place of work, or a voucher for one   s.141(6A)
(eg. an NCP season ticket), whether for an employee's own car or a company car, is
tax free for all employees.

6.2.3   Share options

If an employee is granted the right to acquire shares at an undervalue, he will be   s.135
assessable on the difference between the market value of the shares on the date
they were issued to him and the cost of acquiring the right. Revenue approved
share option schemes receive more favourable treatment. Session 7.3 gives further
details on the taxation of share options.

6.2.4 Accommodation

Basic charge

The value of accommodation provided to any employee (including employees paid £8,500+ and directors) by reason of his employment is the annual value of that property. This is the rent that would have been payable if the premises had been let at their gross annual value (as determined for rating purposes). If the premises are rented rather than owned by the company, then the value to the employee is the higher of the rent actually paid and the gross annual value.

s.145

From 1 April 1990 the rating system for domestic property was replaced by the community charge system and from 1 April 1993 this was replaced by the council tax. As new properties will not therefore be rated it will be necessary for employers to provide an estimate of the gross annual value that would have applied. Where properties already have a gross annual value that value will continue to be used for assessing benefits.

IRPR 19.4.90

The amount assessable on the employee will be reduced by any contribution he makes for the use of the property and any business use element.

Example

Tony is provided with a company flat. For 1996/97 the relevant figures are:

Gross annual (ie. rateable) value	£300
Rent paid by the company	£3,380
Amount paid by Tony to the company for the use of the flat	£520

You are required to show Tony's assessable benefit.

Solution

			£
Benefit: greater of			
- gross annual value ie.	£300		
- rent paid ie.	£3,380		3,380
Less: reimbursed to the company			(520)
Net benefit			£2,860

Job-related accommodation

The employee will not be assessed under Schedule E if the accommodation is provided in one of the following circumstances:

s.145(4)

(a)   residence in the accommodation is necessary for the proper performance of the employee's duties (eg. a caretaker); or

(b)   accommodation is provided for the better performance of the employee's duties and the employment is of a kind in which it is customary for accommodation to be provided (eg. a policeman); or

(c)   the accommodation is provided as part of special security arrangements in force because of a special threat to the employee's security.

In these cases the rental or gross annual value is exempt. An employee in job-related accommodation is not taxed on the benefit of council tax paid directly by the employer.

A director may claim exemption only on the ground in (c) above unless he owns not more than 5% of the shares in the company and either he is a full time working director or the company is established for non-profit making purposes or is a charity.

In this case, a nursery foreman lived three miles from the nursery in a bungalow provided rent-free by his employer. His current employer had purchased the bungalow from his previous employer so that the taxpayer, who could not afford to buy accommodation in the area, could remain in the bungalow. The foreman was on call at all times during the week, and on two weekends out of three. The Revenue included the value of the accommodation, under s.145 ICTA 1988 in his Schedule E assessments. The taxpayer argued that the charge did not apply either because it was 'necessary' or it was 'customary' for his to live in employer's accommodation, and he produced evidence which showed that two thirds of all nursery workers were provided with accommodation.

Vertigan v Brady (1988)

Held: it was not necessary for him to live in the bungalow and that the practice of providing accommodation was not so normal that a custom had become established. The benefit rules applied.

Other exclusions

The employee will also not be assessable under Schedule E if the accommodation is provided by an employer who is an individual and who provides the accommodation in the normal course of his family relationships. He will also not be assessable where the employer is a local authority and the accommodation is not provided on any more favourable terms than to others in similar circumstances.

s.145(7)

Expensive accommodation

Where the cost of the living accommodation exceeds £75,000, an additional benefit in kind will become chargeable upon the employee or director. The additional benefit is found by applying the following formula:

s.146

(Cost of providing living accommodation - £75,000)   x   'the appropriate percentage'

The 'cost of providing' the living accommodation is the aggregate of the cost of purchase and the cost of any improvements made before the relevant tax year. It is therefore *not* possible to avoid the charge by purchasing a property requiring substantial repairs and 'doing it up'. The cost is the net cost, after taking account of any reimbursement of capital expenditure by the employee or any consideration paid by the employee in respect of the grant of a tenancy to him.

If the accommodation was acquired by the employer more than six years before it was first provided to the employee and its original cost plus improvements exceeded £75,000, the 'cost of providing' is increased (or reduced if appropriate) to its market value when first provided to that employee. Note that regardless of current market value, a s.146 charge cannot apply if the original cost plus improvements is under £75,000.

IRPR 18.8.88

The Revenue accept that the £75,000 limit applies property by property, and not to the aggregate of all properties made available to the same employee.

If the employee is exempt from the charge under s.145 he will also be exempt from the additional benefit charge under s.146.

By concession if the s.145 charge is based on the open market rent of the property the employee is exempt from a s.146 charge.

IRPR No.38
28.11.95

IRPR No.38
28.11.95

Although strictly a s.145/s.146 charge could apply separately to each director or employee using the accommodation for the same period, by concession the total is limited to a single charge apportioned fairly between the employee occupiers.

Where any contribution paid by the employee exceeds the annual value of the property, the excess may be deducted from the further benefit.

The 'appropriate percentage' is the same as that used in the beneficial loan rules (see 6.3.8 below). If the rate changes during the tax year, it is the rate at the *start* of the tax year which is used *throughout*.

Example

Simon is provided with a house by his employer (not job-related accommodation). It was originally made available to him on 1 July 1995, although the company had acquired the house, at a cost of £95,000, on 1 April 1992.

On 1 September 1995, £8,000 was spent on extending the property.

For 1996/97, the gross rateable value of the house is £1,400. Simon pays £3,000 for the use of the house to his employer.

You are required to calculate his total benefit for 1996/97 in respect of the house. Apply an official rate of 7.75%.

Solution

	£	£
Basic charge:		
Gross rateable value		1,400
Less: contribution		(1,400)
		nil
Additional charge:		
Cost including improvements		
£95,000 + 8,000	103,000	
Less:	(75,000)	
Excess	£28,000	
£28,000 x 7.75%		2,170
Less: contribution (£3,000 - 1,400)		(1,600)
Total benefit 1996/97		£570

s.146A

From 6 April 1996 it will not be possible to avoid a s.145/146 charge by offering the employee a choice of salary or accommodation. In the past a (lower) cash alternative enabled s.145/146 avoidance.

6.2.5 Mileage allowances

ss197B-197F

There is a statutory scheme which is available to employers who pay mileage allowances to their employees to use their own cars for business travel. This is referred to as the "Fixed Profit Car Scheme" (FPCS).

The tax-free limits are shown on page (ix).

Any amount paid in excess of the limit is a taxable profit in the employee's hands whether he is higher paid or not. Obviously any amount paid to the employee for mileage other than on the employer's business (eg. for home to office mileage) is taxable in full.

The purpose of the higher tax-free rate for the first 4,000 mile band in the statutory FPCS is to provide for recovery of the standing charges which are relatively independent of actual mileage. After that point the mileage rate need only cover the direct costs such as fuel and oil and the marginal extra servicing.

Although the rules are given in statute they are a voluntary alternative to the strict statutory basis. This would involve the employee claiming an allowable deduction under s.198 (see section 6.5) for the business portion of his car running expenses including the interest on any loan taken out to purchase the car and capital allowances for the capital cost of the car.

For 1996/97 onwards an employee who uses his own car for business can use the FPCS rates to calculate his profits or, if appropriate, make a claim for a tax deduction.

Example

Owen drives 9,000 business miles in 1996/97 using his own 1600 cc car.

You are required to calculate the taxable profit/allowable expense assuming:

(a) He is reimbursed 40p a mile

(b) He is reimbursed 25p a mile

(c) No reimbursement is made.

Solution

			£
FPCS limit:	4,000 x 43p		1,720
	5,000 x 23p		1,150
			2,870
a)	Profit: 40p x 9,000 = 3,600 - 2,870		£730
b)	Expense claim: 2,870 - (9,000 x 25p = 2,250)		£620
c)	Expense claim:		£2,870

6.3 Benefits in kind assessable on employees paid £8,500 or more and directors

6.3.1 Employees paid £8,500 or more and directors

The extent to which an employee is assessed on benefits in kind, and the rules of assessment applied, depend on whether or not he is an employee paid £8,500+ pa. (or a director).

'Emoluments' for the £8,500 pa. test include salary, commissions, fees, reimbursed expenses and also benefits in kind assessable on employees paid £8,500+ pa./directors. In other words, one must *initially assume* that a particular employee is paid £8,500 pa. or more in order to determine whether or not he really is in that category.
You may find it useful to learn the following pro-forma:

s.167

	£
Salary (net of pension contributions)	X
Commissions	X
Fees	X
Reimbursed expenses	X
Benefits assessable on employees paid £8,500 pa. or more	X
TEST HERE	X
Less: allowable deductions	(X)
Assessment if the taxpayer is paid £8,500 pa. or more	£X

Note that the test must be made before making allowance for any deductions (eg. expenses).

A 'director' is assessed to benefits in kind in the same way as an employee paid over £8,500 pa. The term 'director' refers to any person who acts as a director or any person in accordance with whose instructions the directors are accustomed to act (other than a professional advisor). Excluded, however, is any director who is a full-time working director, or a director of a non-profit making company or charity, and who, with associates, controls not more than 5% of the voting rights of the company. Such a person will, however, be subject to the special benefits rules if he earns £8,500 pa. or more.

s.168(8)&(9)

6.3.2 The general rule

Generally, any benefits in kind for employees paid £8,500 pa. and directors are assessable on the *cost of providing* the benefit rather than on second hand value. Thus, for example, medical insurance is caught, even though it cannot be re-sold at all. But again, the legislation provides special rules in a number of specific instances. You should also note that a benefit arises if it is provided 'by reason of the employment'. There is no need for the employer to provide it directly. Also the benefit does not have to be provided to the employee or director. The rules apply equally if benefits are provided to members of his family or household.

s.154(1)

Where in-house benefits are provided, this case established that the cost of providing the benefit (and therefore the benefit in kind) is the marginal cost and not the average cost. This case involved employees of a public school paying much reduced fees for having their own children educated at the school. The fee was calculated to cover the extra cost to the school eg. food and laundry from admitting the employee's child. As the staff were merely taking up places which would otherwise go unused they argued (successfully) that there was no cost to the employer as they had reimbursed the marginal (ie. additional) costs. The Revenue had wanted to value the benefit by averaging the total school costs over the total number of pupils. This marginal cost basis is relevant to a wide range of employments and can apply, for example, where employees of transport undertakings are allowed to take up unsold seats free or at below the full price.

Pepper v Hart (1992)

6.3.3   Expenses connected with living accommodation

In addition to the benefit on the living accommodation itself which is taxable on all employees, there is also a benefit for employees paid £8,500 p.a. or more and directors, taxing related expenses such as:

s.163

(a)   heating, lighting or cleaning the premises;

(b)   repairing, maintaining or decorating them;

(c)   providing furniture etc. normal for domestic occupation (annual value taken as 20% of cost - see para 6.3.7 below).

Unless the accommodation qualifies as 'job-related' (as defined in paragraph 6.2.4 above) the full cost of ancillary services (excluding structural repairs) is assessable. If the accommodation is 'job-related', however, the assessment for ancillary services is restricted to a maximum of 10% of the 'net emoluments'. For this purpose, net emoluments are all amounts taxable under Schedule E (excluding the ancillary benefits (a) - (c) above) less any allowable expenses, contributions to approved pension schemes, retirement annuity contracts and personal pension plans, and capital allowances. If there are ancillary benefits other than those falling within (a) - (c) above (eg. a telephone) they are taxable in full.

Example

> Mr. Quinton is employed as a security guard, earning £13,000 in 1996/97. In order to carry out his duties properly he is required to live in a house adjacent to his employer's premises and this is accepted by the Revenue as job-related accommodation. The house cost £70,000 two years ago. The gross annual value of the house is £650. The company pays in 1996/97 an electricity bill of £250, a gas bill of £200, a gardener's bill of £150 and redecoration costs of £1,000. Mr Quinton makes a monthly contribution of £50 for his accommodation. He also pays 5% of his salary as superannuation contributions and drives a company car on which the assessable benefit is £2,990 (see paragraph 6.3.4).

> **You are required to calculate the amount assessable under Schedule E for 1996/97.**

Solution

	£	£
Salary		13,000
Car benefit		2,990
		15,990
Less: superannuation contributions 5% x £13,000		(650)
Net emoluments		15,340
Accommodation benefits:		
Gross annual value - exempt		
Ancillary services:		
Electricity	250	
Gas	200	
Gardener	150	
Redecorations	1,000	
	1,600	
Restricted to 10% of £15,340	1,534	
Less: employee's contribution	(600)	934
Assessable under Schedule E		£16,274

6.3.4 The car benefit rules

Special rules apply for taxing car benefits enjoyed by employees paid £8,500 pa. or more and directors.   s.157 and Sch 6

(a)   The tax charge arises whether the car is provided by the employer or by some other person

(b)   The benefit chargeable to tax each year is basically 35% of the car's price

(c)   The price of the car is the sum of the following items:

   (i)   The list price of the car for a single retail sale in the UK at the time of first registration, including charges for delivery and standard accessories. A notional list price is estimated if no list price was published

   (ii)   The price (including fitting) of all optional accessories provided when the car was first provided to the employee, excluding mobile telephones

   (iii)   The price (including fitting) of all optional accessories fitted later and costing at least £100 each, excluding mobile telephones. Such accessories affect the taxable benefit from and including the year of assessment in which they are fitted. However, accessories which are merely replacing existing accessories and are not superior to the ones replaced are ignored

Example

Frank Ord is provided on 6 April 1996 with a Mondeo which, with optional extras, had a list price of £18,200. His employer had only paid £16,800 being a fleet purchaser.

Frank's car benefit for 1996/97 is 35% x £18,200 = £6,370

(d)   There is a special rule for classic cars. If the car is at least 15 years old (from the time of first registration) at the end of the year of assessment, and its market value at the end of the year (or, if earlier, when it ceased to be available to the employee) is over £15,000 and greater than the price found under (c), that market value is used instead of the price. The market value takes account of all accessories (except mobile telephones).

(e)   If the price or value found under (c) or (d) exceeds £80,000, then £80,000 is used instead of the price or value.

(f)   If the employee makes a capital contribution towards the cost of the car or accessories this is deducted from the price for calculating the benefit, subject to a maximum deduction of £5,000.

(g)   The basic charge is reduced by $1/3$ or $2/3$ dependent on the *business* mileage in the tax year, see page (ix).

If a further car or cars is also provided, there is no reduction for mileage up to 18,000 miles. There is a $1/3$ reduction for business miles of 18,000 or more. The car with the greatest business mileage is treated as the main car.

All motoring is private except that which a person is necessarily obliged to do in the performance of the duties of his employment. Travel between home and work is only business travel if the employee has a travelling appointment (as with a travelling salesperson), the employee is travelling to a temporary place of work which is closer to his home than to his normal place of work, or the employee's home counts as a place of work.

(h)   If the car is at least four years old (from the date of first registration) at the end of the year of assessment, the benefit otherwise calculated is reduced as shown on page (ix).

Example

Nigel Issan is provided with a car which had a list price of £22,000 when it was first registered in August 1992. He drives 21,000 miles a year of which about 80% is on business.

You are required to calculate Nigel's car benefit for 1996/97.

Solution

		£
List price	£22,000 x 35%	7,700
Less:	1/3 reduction for mileage	(2,567)
		5,133
Less:	1/3 reduction for age	
	£5,133 x 1/3	(1,711)
Car benefit		£3,422

(i)   The benefit is reduced on a time basis where a car is first made available or ceases to be made available during the year or is incapable of being used for a continuous period of not less than 30 days (for example because it is being repaired). The mileage factor limits of 2,500 and 18,000 miles are also reduced on a time basis in such cases. If a car is unavailable for less than 30 days and a replacement car of similar quality is provided, the replacement car is ignored and business mileage in it counts as business mileage in the usual car.

Example

Vicky Olvo starts her employment on 6 January 1997 and is immediately provided with a new car with a list price of £25,000. The car was more expensive than her employer would have provided and she therefore made a capital contribution of £6,200. Business mileage up to 5 April was 5,200 and she contributed £100 a month for being able to use the car privately.

You are required to calculate her car benefit for 1996/97.

Solution

		£
Price		25,000
Less:	capital contributions (maximum)	(5,000)
		20,000

		£
"List price" £20,000 x 35%		7,000
Less:	2/3rd reduction for mileage *	(4,667)
		£2,333

		£
3/12 x £2,333 **		583
Less:	contribution to running costs £100 x 3	(300)
Car benefit		£283

* 5,200 for 3 months = 20,800 pa > 18,000
** Only available for 3 months in 1996/97

(j) The benefit is reduced by any payment the user must make for the private use of the car (as distinct from a capital contribution to the cost of the car). However, the benefit cannot become negative to create a deduction from the employee's income.

(k) Pool cars are exempt. A car only qualifies as a pool car if *all* the following conditions are satisfied.

 (i) It is used by more than one director or employee and is not ordinarily used by any one of them to the exclusion of the others.

 (ii) Any private use is merely incidental to business use.

 (iii) It is not normally kept overnight at or near the residence of a director or employee.

(l) Where an employee has sacrificed salary to obtain private use of a car, the taxable benefit will be the higher of salary foregone, or the benefit calculated as above.

s.157A

Employers must make quarterly returns of any changes in cars provided to employees on form P46 (car). These returns are made for income tax quarters (ending on 5 July, 5 October, 5 January and 5 April), and must be made within 28 days of the end of each quarter.

The benefit calculated as above taxes the benefit of 'a car...made available ... for ... private use'. This covers all expenditure by the employer on repairs, servicing, insurance, road fund licence and cleaning. It does not cover the cost of a chauffeur. Where a chauffeur is provided for both business and private mileage, an agreed proportion of the employer's associated costs would be assessable on the employee. Note that there are special rules for taxing mobile telephones including car telephones (see 6.3.5 below).

SP 5/88

Fuel benefit

Where fuel for private motoring is provided to an employee paid £8,500 pa. or more or a director in a company car he will be assessed on a fuel benefit in addition to the car benefit mentioned above dependent on whether the fuel used is diesel or petrol. Fuel benefits are shown on page (ix).

No benefit in kind is levied where it can be shown that either all the fuel provided was used only for business travel or that the employee is required to (and has) made good the whole of the expense of any fuel provided for his private use. It should be noted that, unlike the position with most benefits, a reimbursement of only part of the cost of the fuel available for private use will not result in any reduction of the assessable benefit. The fuel benefit is thus an 'all or nothing' charge.

Unlike the car benefit there are no adjustments for the fuel benefit for significant or high business mileages, or where the car is a second or subsequent car, or where the car is over four years old.

The fuel benefit charge only applies in conjunction with a company car. If fuel is provided for an employee's own car, the normal rule of 'cost of providing' applies.

Example

An employee was provided with a new car (2.8 litres) costing £15,000 including VAT on 6 June 1996. During 1996/97 the employer spent £900 on insurance, repairs and vehicle licence. The employee drove the car 20,000 miles of which 17,000 were on business. The firm paid for all petrol (£2,300) without reimbursement. The employee was required to pay the firm £270 for the private use of the car.

You are required to calculate the total assessable benefit for 1996/97 in respect of the car and fuel.

Solution

Car less than 4 years old and available for 10 months. Mileage limit 18,000 x 10/12 = 15,000 exceeded.

	£
List price £15,000 x 35%	5,250
Less: 2/3 reduction for mileage	(3,500)
	£1,750

	£
£1,750 x $^{10}/_{12}$	1,458
Less contribution	(270)
	1,188
Fuel benefit £1,320 x 10/12	1,100
Assessable benefit	£2,288

If the contribution of £270 had been towards the petrol the benefit assessable would have been £2,558. Conversely, if the cost of private petrol were fully reimbursed by the employee (say - £2,300 x 3,000/20,000 ie. £345) then there would have been no fuel benefit at all. The employer must account for VAT on the employee's contribution and it is understood that the entire employee contribution (ie. the VAT inclusive amount) is deductible in calculating the benefit.

Note that no benefit arises on the provision of a car parking space.   s.197A

6.3.5   Mobile telephones

Mobile telephones are the subject of a standard charge of £200 pa. each where   s.159A
provided as a benefit to an employee, whether or not fixed in a company car.

The charge for a mobile telephone is reduced by any contribution required from the employee for private use. The charge is cancelled if there is no private use or if the employee is required to and does repay the whole cost of any private use, including the appropriate portion of subscriber charges and other standing costs such as maintenance contract charges.

6.3.6   Company vans

A standard annual charge of £500 applies to an employee who has any private   ss.159AA to
use of a van provided by his employer. This only applies to vans with a gross   159AC and Sch
vehicle weight of 3.5 tonnes or less - although a van over that weight will attract   6A
a standard charge if it is used *wholly or mainly* for the employee's private
purposes.

If the van is over 4 years old by the end of the year of assessment the annual charge is reduced to £350.

As for company cars, the charge is pro-rated if the van is only provided for part of the year or if it is incapable of being used for 30 or more consecutive days. The charge is also reduced by any contributions made by the employee to the employer for private use.

If an employee has the use of more than one van over the same period a charge will be made for each van. If a van is available for private use for two or more employees over the same period the charge (£500 or £350) is shared between them. As for cars, it is possible to claim "pooled van" status, thereby avoiding the charge. There will be a "pooled van" if the use of a van is shared, if any private use is incidental and if the van is not normally kept at or near the homes of the employees who share its use.

Unlike the rules for cars, the van charge includes the benefit of any fuel provided by the employer for private use. If no charge applies because the van's weight exceeds 3.5 tonnes, no charge will arise on the provision of fuel for private use.

6.3.7   Other assets available for private use

Assets made available for the use of employees paid £8,500+ p.a. and directors   s.156
are taxable on an annual value equal to 20% of the market value when first
applied as a benefit to any employee or at the rental paid by the employer if
higher.

In addition, a benefit arises on any other expenses incurred in connection with the provision of the asset, eg. for its maintenance.

If an asset made available is subsequently acquired by the employee, the assessable benefit on the acquisition is the greater of:

(a)   the excess of the current market value over the price paid by the employee; and

(b)   the excess of market value when first provided less any amounts already assessed as a benefit over the price paid by the employee.

This rule prevents tax free benefits arising on fast depreciating items by the employee purchasing them at a much reduced second-hand value.

Example

A suit costing £200 is purchased by an employer for use by an employee on 6 April 1995. On 6 April 1996 the suit is purchased by the employee for £15, its market value then being £25.

The benefit assessable in 1995/96 will be 20% x £200			£40
			£
The benefit assessable in 1996/97 will be the greater of:			
(a)	Market value at acquisition by employee		25
	Less: price paid		(15)
			£10
			£
(b)	Original market value		200
	Less: assessed in respect of use		(40)
			160
	Less: price paid		(15)
Benefit (since greater than £10)			£145

Provided the employee does not acquire the ownership of the asset, he will only be assessed on 20% of original value each year (even for more than five years if the use continues). It is still tax efficient for assets like suits which need replacing every two or three years to be purchased by the employer rather than by the employee out of net income.

6.3.8   Beneficial loans

Loans to employees, directors and their families give rise to Schedule E emoluments equal to: s.160

(a)   any amounts written off (unless the employee has died); and

(b)   the excess of the interest based on an official rate prescribed by the Treasury over any interest actually charged. Interest payable during the tax year but paid after the end of the tax year is taken into account, but if the benefit is determined before such interest is paid a claim must be made to take it into account.

The following loans are ignored altogether for the purposes of computing taxable income because of low interest (but not for the purposes of the charge on loans written off).   s.161

(a)   A loan made in the ordinary course of the employer's money-lending business, provided that all of the following conditions are satisfied.

(i)   When the loan was made, comparable loans (that is, loans for the same or similar purposes, and on the same terms and conditions) were available to all potential customers

(ii)   A substantial proportion of comparable loans made at about the same time were to members of the public

(iii) The loan to the director or employee and loans made to the public at about the same time continue to be on the same terms, with any changes to the terms having been imposed in the ordinary course of business

(b) A loan made by an individual in the ordinary course of the lender's domestic, family or personal arrangements

Calculating the interest benefit

There are two alternative methods of calculating the amount of the benefit to be assessed to tax. The simpler 'average' method is applied automatically unless an election is made by the taxpayer or the Revenue. (The Revenue normally only make the election where it appears that the 'average' method is being deliberately exploited.) In both methods, the benefit is the interest at the official rate minus the interest payable.

Sch.7

The election can be made during the period starting with 31 January following the tax year and ending twelve months thereafter.

The first method averages the balances at the beginning and end of the year of assessment (or the dates on which the loan was made and discharged if it was not in existence throughout the year) and applies the official rate of interest to this average. If the loan was not in existence throughout the year only the number of complete tax months (from the 6th of the month) for which it existed are taken into account.

The second method is to compute interest at the official rate on a daily basis on the actual amount outstanding.

For 1996/97 onwards different loans to the same employee are usually treated separately. The lender can elect to aggregate certain loans before the end of the period of 92 days after the end of the tax year, where the loans are to a director of a close company. Before 1996/97 all loans to the same employee were always treated as a single loan.

s.160(1B) & (1BA)

Example

At 6 April 1996 a low interest loan of £30,000 was outstanding to an employee earning £12,000 a year, who repaid £20,000 on 7 December 1996. The remaining balance of £10,000 was outstanding at 5 April 1997. Interest paid during the year was £250. What was the benefit under both methods for 1996/97, assuming that the official rate of interest was 7.75% until 5 August 1996 and 9% thereafter?

Solution

Average method

	£
$7.75\% \times \dfrac{30,000 + 10,000}{2} \times {}^4/_{12}$	517
$9\% \times \dfrac{30,000 + 10,000}{2} \times {}^8/_{12}$	1,200
	1,717
Less: interest paid	(250)
Assessable benefit	£1,467

Alternative method

	£
£30,000 $\times \dfrac{122}{365}$ (6 April - 5 August 1996) x 7.75%	777
£30,000 $\times \dfrac{123}{365}$ (6 August - 6 December 1996) x 9%	910
£10,000 $\times \dfrac{120}{365}$ (7 December 1996 - 5 April 1997) x 9%	296
	1,983
Less: interest paid	(250)
Assessable benefit	£1,733

The Revenue will opt for the alternative method if they think that the rules of the average method are being deliberately exploited.

The de minimis test

The benefit is not treated as emoluments in either of the following cases.

s.161

(a)   The total balance on all loans to the employee did not exceed £5,000 at any time in the year.

(b)   The loan is not a qualifying loan and the balance on all non-qualifying loans to the employee did not exceed £5,000 at any time in the year.

A qualifying loan is one on which any interest would qualify as a charge or as a tax reducer (disregarding the £30,000 limit on loans where interest qualifies as a tax reducer).

In applying the £5,000 test, ignore any loans which are to be ignored under the rules relating to loans in the ordinary course of a money-lending business or of domestic, family, or personal arrangements.

When the £5,000 threshold is exceeded, a benefit arises on interest on the whole loan, not just on the excess of the loan over £5,000.

When a loan is written off and a benefit arises, there is no £5,000 threshold: writing off a loan of £1 gives rise to a £1 benefit.

Qualifying loans

When an employee is treated as receiving emoluments because the actual rate of interest is below the official rate, he is also treated as paying interest equal to the emoluments. This amount may then qualify as a charge or (subject to the usual £30,000 limit) as a tax reducer, in addition to any interest actually paid.

Example

Anna, who is single, has an annual salary of £30,000 and two loans from her employer.

(a)   A season ticket loan of £2,300 at no interest

(b)   A house purchase loan (not under MIRAS) of £54,000 at 3% interest

The official rate of interest is to be taken as 7.75%.

What is Anna's tax liability for 1996/97?

Solution

	£
Salary	30,000
Season ticket loan: not over £5,000	nil
House purchase loan £54,000 x (7.75 - 3)%	2,565
Schedule E	32,565
Less: personal allowance	(3,765)
Taxable income	£28,800

Income tax	£
£3,900 x 20%	780
£21,600 x 24%	5,184
£3,300 x 40%	1,320
	7,284
Less: tax reduction £30,000 (limit) x (4.75 + 3)% x 15%	(349)
Tax borne and tax payable	£6,935

Mr Todd, as district inspector of taxes in Wigan, was required to move to London. His employer provided him with an interest-free advance of salary of £8,440. The advance was repayable on demand, but would be recovered by monthly deductions from his salary over a ten year period. Mr Todd was assessed to income tax under Schedule E on the cash equivalent of the benefit of the loan under s.160 ICTA 1988.

Williams v Todd (1988)

Held: despite the taxpayer's argument that the advance was not a loan, and that he derived no benefit from it, the court upheld the assessment.

6.4 Tax-free benefits - summary

There is a fairly long list of benefits which are *non-taxable* on *all* employees, including:

(a) accommodation and subsistence:

   (i) living accommodation which constitutes job-related accommodation (see para 6.2.4.);

   (ii) meals in a staff canteen, provided that they are available to all employees on broadly similar terms;   s.155(5) ESC A74

   (iii) the first 15p per working day of luncheon vouchers;   ESC A2

   (iv) personal incidental expenses of up to £5 per night for employees working away from home in the UK, or £10 per night if working abroad which would otherwise be taxable. (eg. laundry, newspapers, telephone calls home).   s.200A

However, where more than one night is spent away, the exemption works on an aggregate basis eg. for four nights the overall limit is £20.   IRPR 16.5.95

(b) travel:

   (i) the provision of a car parking space at or near the place of work;   s.197A

   (ii) fixed profit car scheme; or mileage allowances, up to reasonable limits;   s197B-F

   (iii) a payment for additional transport costs or the cost of overnight accommodation in a case where public transport is disrupted by industrial action;   ESC A58

   (iv) a payment for a taxi or hired car for an employee who is occasionally required to work late (after 9pm), in circumstances where either public transport has ceased or it would be unreasonable to expect the employee to use it. If such arrangements occur frequently (more than 60 times a year) or regularly (eg. every Friday), then *no* exemption is available;   ESC A66

   (v) the reimbursement to a director or employee of costs necessarily incurred in travelling to another company in the same group of which he is a director;   ESC A4

(c) education and training:

   (i) certain payments made by an employer to an employee for attendance at a full-time training course (including a sandwich course) at a university, college, school or similar establishment;   SP 4/86

   (ii) payments made in respect of a past or present employee for the costs of a qualifying training or retraining course - full time, day release or block release;   ss.588 & 589 ESC A63 & A64

(d) removal expenses:

up to £8,000 of removal expenses borne by the employer where the employee has to move house on first taking up the employment or on a transfer within the organisation. "Removal expenses" include for this purpose the reimbursement of *net* interest (ie. after tax relief) on a bridging loan, usual professional fees, costs of finding a new home, and replacement of curtains and carpets;   Sch 11A

(e)   entertainment:

(i)   the provision of a Christmas party or alternative function, provided that the cost is no more than £75 per head;   ESC A70

(ii)   the provision of entertainment by a person who is neither the employer, nor connected with the employer (see para 6.2.2);   s.141 (6B)
                                                                                                                                           s.142 (3B)
                                                                                                                                           s.155 (7)

(f)   child care facilities:

child care facilities either on the employer's premises or on other premises where the employer is at least partly responsible for the financing and management of the facilities. The premises must be non-domestic; the child must be under eighteen and under the parental responsibility of the employee (so could include a foster child); and any legal conditions for running a nursery must be satisfied. "Care" can include after school or holiday supervision but excludes supervision which is primarily educational. Relief does not extend to providing nursery vouchers or reimbursing the employee's child minder costs;   s.155A

(g)   miscellaneous :

(i)   long service awards - for service in excess of 20 years, £20 per year of service is tax-free;   ESC A22

(ii)   miner's free coal or cash in-lieu allowance;   ESC A6

(iii)   awards under a formally constituted staff suggestion scheme;   ESC A57

(iv)   gifts (other than cash) received by reason of the employment from someone other than the employer, provided that they amount to less than £150 in a tax year from a particular source;   ESC A70

(v)   overseas medical expenses incurred whilst working abroad as part of the duties of the employment, and the cost of insuring against such expenses;   ss.155(6)

(vi)   assets or services provided to improve an employee's personal physical security from a threat arising out of his employment.   FA 1989 ss.50-52

(vii)   workplace sports or recreational facilities provided by employers for use by their staff generally. This does not apply where the employer pays or reimburses an employee's subscription to a sports club nor where the facilities are only available to limited groups of employees;   s.197G

(viii) air miles and car fuel coupons obtained in the course of business travel;

(ix)   premiums providing for liabilities and indemnities insurance cover for directors and employees; expenditure in discharging an employee's liabilities incurred in his capacity as employee; and costs of proceedings relating to such matters (Any such costs paid by an employee qualify for tax relief.);   s.201AA

(x)   contributions to an approved occupational, or personal pension scheme.

(xi)   travel and subsistence payments made to Government ministers or members of their families or households. This does not apply to the provision of mobile phones.   s.200 AA

The above list is not exhaustive, but provides a reasonably comprehensive summary of the tax free benefits of which you need to be aware.

6.5 Allowable deductions

6.5.1 Introduction

Four types of expenditure are specifically deductible against Schedule E expenditure. These are:

(a) contributions (within certain limits) to an approved occupational pension scheme;

(b) premiums paid (within certain limits) for approved retirement annuity contracts or personal pension plans;

(c) subscriptions to professional bodies, if relevant to the duties; and   s.201

(d) donations to charity (up to £1,200 pa.) under an approved payroll   s.202
deduction scheme.

Otherwise, claims for deductions against Schedule E income are notoriously hard to obtain. When they are obtained, they fall into the following categories:

(a) travel expenses incurred *necessarily in* the performance of the duties;   s.198

(b) other expenses incurred *wholly, exclusively and necessarily in* the performance of the duties; and

(c) capital allowances on plant and machinery (other than a car) *necessarily*   s.27(2)CAA 1990
provided for use *in* the performance of the duties, and capital allowances   s.27(2A) to (2E)
on a car provided by the employee for use in the performance of the duties   CAA 1990
(ie. no *necessarily* test for cars).

Note that the word 'necessarily' is particularly restrictive. Schedule D Case I expenses have to satisfy only a 'wholly and exclusively' test and are, therefore, much more likely to be allowable. This partly explains why taxpayers prefer to be self-employed rather than employed.

6.5.2 Deductions for travelling expenses

Expenditure 'in the performance of' duties does not include expenditure incurred in order to get into a position to perform duties. Thus travel to work is not allowable.

The types of expenditure which may be deducted rests largely on case law.

A barrister practising in London was appointed Recorder of Portsmouth. He   Ricketts v
claimed travelling expenses.   Colquhoun
(1935)

Held: disallowable since the duties were carried out in Portsmouth not London, hence the expenses were not incurred 'in the performance of' the duties.

A part time hospital consultant claimed travel costs to and from the hospital   Pook v Owen
since his duties began when he received a telephone call from the hospital.   (1969)

Held: the costs were allowed since the doctor was considered to have two places of work - his surgery and the hospital. These duties began in the surgery when the telephone rang.

A doctor in general practice held three part-time Schedule E appointments at   Parikh v Sleeman
hospitals. He claimed as an allowable expense the costs of travelling to and   (1988)
between the hospitals at which he was employed.

Held: the expenses were neither incurred necessarily nor incurred in the performance of the duties, and were not allowable.

A taxpayer who was employed by his own company operating from his home address could not deduct, from his remuneration as a director, the cost of travelling to work at the location of a client 80 miles away. This was on the basis that the directorial duties need not have been carried out at the home address rather than anywhere else and so the expenses were not necessarily incurred in the performance of his duties.

Miners v Atkinson (1995)

6.5.3 Other expense claims

The word 'exclusively' strictly implies that the expenditure should give no private benefit at all. If it does, none of it is deductible. In practice inspectors will sometimes ignore a small element of private benefit or make an apportionment between business and private use.

Whether the expense is 'necessary' is not determined by what the employer requires. The test is whether the duties of the employment cannot be performed without the outlay. It is an objective, not a subjective test.

A local government officer claimed as an allowable expense the cost of evening meals taken when attending late meetings.

Sanderson v Durbridge (1955)

Held: not allowed since not incurred in the performance of the duties.

An airline pilot was liable to be called for duty at any time. He claimed a deduction for:

Nolder v Walters (1930)

(a) travel to the airport;

(b) telephone;

(c) subsistence whilst abroad in excess of his employer's allowance.

Held: (a) and (b) were disallowed since not necessarily incurred in the performance of the duties. (c) was allowed as his duties included the return journey, and the expense was therefore in the performance of those duties.

As a condition of his employment as a laboratory assistant an employee was required to study for a degree by attending evening classes. He claimed the cost of his textbooks and travel.

Blackwell v Mills (1945)

Held: not allowable since not expenditure in the performance of the duties.

A solicitor's articled clerk claimed the cost of his exam fees.

Lupton v Potts (1969)

Held: not allowed since neither wholly nor exclusively incurred in the performance of his duties, rather in furthering the clerk's ambition to become a solicitor.

The manager of a West End bank claimed the expense of joining a club since this was virtually a requisite of the employment.

Brown v Bullock (1961)

Held: since it would have been possible to carry on the employment without the club membership the expense was not necessary and therefore disallowed.

A managing director's subscriptions to two residential London clubs were claimed by him as an expense on the grounds that they were cheaper than hotels.

Elwood v Utitz (1965)

Held: the expenditure was allowed. It was necessary in that it would be impossible for the employee to carry out his London duties without him being provided with first class accommodation. The cheaper residential facilities were given to club members only.

While working away from home as an inspector for a firm of consulting engineers, Mr Hindmarsh received a weekly allowance to cover his living expenses. he spent periods varying from a few days to two months at different sites. Tax was charged under Schedule E on the living allowance, but his claim to deduct the expenses under s.198 ICTA 1988 failed.

Elderkin v Hindmarsh (1988)

It could not be said that the expenses were incurred 'in the performance of' the duties of the office. He started work when he arrived at the site and finished when the day's work was over. He did not live in the accommodation in the course of performing his duties.

Journalists purchased newspapers and periodicals out of an allowance paid to them by their employer, in order to keep up to date. The journalists claimed a deduction under s.198 ICTA 1988.

Fitzpatrick & Others v IRC (1994) Smith v Abbot & others (1994)

Held: the journalists were preparing themselves to carry out the duties of their employment, rather than carrying out the performance of their duties, as required by s.198.

6.6 Payments on termination of employment

Payments on termination of employment fall into one of three categories for taxation purposes:

(a) entirely exempt payments;

(b) partially exempt payments; and

(c) entirely chargeable payments.

The following types of payment on termination of employment are specifically exempt by statute:

s.188(1)

(a) a payment on death;

(b) a payment on account of injury or disability;

(c) a lump sum payment from an approved pension scheme;

(d) legal costs recovered by the employee from the employer following legal action to recover compensation for loss of employment, where the costs are ordered by the court or (for out-of-court settlements) are paid directly to the employee's solicitor as part of the settlement.

By contrast, a termination payment not falling within (a) to (d) above but which is made *in return for services* will be fully taxable under normal Schedule E rules. The question of whether a payment is made in return for services can be a complex one, but generally, if the contract of employment provides for payment to be made on termination (or indeed variation of the terms) of employment, the payment will be in return for services. If the contract is silent on this point but a payment is made, it will be taken to be in return for services if there was a reasonable expectation that such a sum would be paid. Accordingly, these payments made in return for services are taxed in full under Schedule E.

Other payments on termination (such as compensation for loss of office and including statutory redundancy pay), which are not taxable under the normal Schedule E rules because they are not in return for services, are nevertheless brought under the Schedule E regime by s.148 ICTA 1988.

s.580(3)
s.148

Termination payments subject to s.148 are however partially exempt: the first £30,000 is free of income tax.

s.188

The cost of outplacement services incurred by the employer for the employee's benefit is exempt and does not reduce the £30,000 exempt amount.

s.598A(4)

When considering the date on which a non-exempt termination payment should be taxed (and therefore possibly which tax year it falls into) the important date is that on which the employment was *terminated*. The date the money is received is irrelevant, contrary to the usual rule. Remember that the payment could include non-cash items, such as a car, which should be brought into account at market value.

Further exemptions may be available if the employee's period of service includes foreign service - see Session 8.

Although the receipts basis does not apply to termination payments, it does apply to normal emoluments which are paid after employment has ceased (or before employment has commenced for that matter) - see para 6.1.2.

The Revenue treat termination payments made on the employee's retirement as "relevant benefits" as defined in s.612 ICTA 1988. Since they are deemed to arise from an unapproved retirement benefit scheme, they become taxable under Schedule E under s.596A ICTA 1988 and therefore do not qualify for the £30,000 exemption available under s.148 ICTA 1988.

However, the Pension Schemes Office (PSO) will approve an ex-gratia lump sum relevant benefit (ie. allow it to be tax free) if there is no other approved scheme from which the employee could obtain a tax free lump sum and if the sum falls within the normal approved limits. These are 3/80 of final salary for each year of service with the employer (maximum 40). In addition, there will be automatic approval for 'small' payments - less than $1/12$ of the "earnings cap" for the year (£82,200 for 1996/97 - see paragraph 5.9.2).

SP 13/91

The Revenue have commented that they will not give "hard and fast rules" on whether a situation amounts to retirement. They concede that a man of middle years moving on to further full-time employment is obviously not retiring but that they are likely to apply the "relevant benefit" rule to a man of older years who has no other full-time employment in prospect.

Law Society
memo dated
7.10.92

This is not much help in practice for the many situations in between. However, an exam question on this topic should make it clear whether the termination amounts to retirement. If it does not, you must state any assumption you have made to resolve the ambiguity.

An interesting case concerns Peter Shilton, the ex-England goalkeeper. Shilton was employed by Nottingham Forest Football Club and an agreement was reached to transfer him to Southampton. Nottingham Forest paid Shilton £75,000 and the inspector assessed this to Schedule E under s.19(1) ICTA 1988. Shilton claimed that it was a *termination payment* under s.148, and eligible for relief under s.188. The Revenue argued that the payment by Nottingham Forest was an *inducement* to Shilton to play for Southampton and therefore an emolument deriving from his contract with Southampton, and so liable under s.19(1) and s.131(1), rather than s.148.

Shilton v
Wilmshurst
(1991)

Held: s.19(1) was not confined to 'emoluments from an employer' but embraced all 'emoluments from employment'. In other words, emoluments provided by third parties are taxable within s.19(1). The effect of the arrangement was that the £75,000 was an inducement payment from Southampton, which was actually paid by a third party (Nottingham Forest). As an inducement payment taxable under s.19(1) it was not caught by the termination payments legislation and therefore the s.188 exemption was not available.

QUESTIONS

1. Describe the basis of assessment under Schedule E.

2. Someone is regarded as self-employed if he has a contract........., whereas if he has a contract......, he will be regarded as an employee. Fill in the missing words.

3. An employee is provided with a flat by his employer (not job-related accommodation). The rateable value of the flat is £400; rent paid by the employer amounts to £3,900 per annum.

   How much is included in the employee's emoluments in respect of this benefit?

4. The additional charge on "expensive" accommodation (costing more than £75,000) applies only to employees paid £8,500+ p.a. and directors. TRUE/FALSE?

5. Is Megan an employee paid £8,500+ p.a. in 1996/97?

	£
Salary	5,560
Charge re company car (assuming 'higher paid')	2,310
Reimbursed expenses (of which 75% are deductible)	880

6. Is the fuel scale benefit reduced by any reimbursement by the employee of the cost of fuel provided for private mileage?

7. A video recorder costing £500 was made available to Gordon by his employer on 6 April 1995. On 6 April 1996, Gordon bought the recorder for £150, when its market value was £325. What assessable benefit arises in 1996/97 if Gordon's salary amounts to £15,000 per annum?

8. The first £500 notional interest on an interest-free loan is exempt from tax. TRUE/FALSE?

9. How much of a termination payment, brought within the charge to Schedule E by virtue only of s.148 ICTA 1988, is exempt from tax?

10. Buster is the Managing Director of Buster Braces Ltd and is supplied with a vintage Bentley (3 litre, petrol engine) which originally cost £900 in 1932 but was purchased by the company for £82,000 in 1995 and is still worth that much. He was disqualified for dangerous driving so is supplied with a chauffeur at the company's expense (full salary costs for 1996/97 - £13,500). In 1996/97 the car is used 3,000 miles for business out of a total mileage of 12,000. The car is fitted with a telephone which Buster uses both for business and privately. All running costs are borne by the company. What is the total benefit in kind?

SOLUTIONS

1. Schedule E assesses the amount received during the year of assessment, regardless of when it is earned (6.1.2).

2. Self employed: contract *for services*

   Employee: contract *of service*

   (6.1.3).

3. £3,900, being the higher of the rateable value and rent actually paid (6.2.4).

4. FALSE. Only those in occupation of "job-related" accommodation can avoid the additional charge

   (6.2.4).

5. YES

		£
Emoluments:	Salary	5,560
	Car benefit	2,310
	Reimbursed expenses	880
	TEST HERE (>£8,500)	8,750
	Less: allowable expenses (£880 x 75%)	(660)
	ASSESSMENT	£8,090

   (6.3.1)

6. Not unless the employer is fully reimbursed, in which case the fuel benefit is nil (6.3.4).

7. Benefit is based on the higher of:

(a)	Current MV		£325
(b)	Original MV	£500	
	Less: already assessed (in 1995/96)		
	£500 x 20%	(100)	£400

   ie. £400

   Therefore the assessable benefit after deduction of the amount paid (£150) is £250.

   (6.3.7).

8. FALSE - only if the loan does not exceed £5,000 is it ignored (6.3.8).

9. £30,000 (6.6).

10.

	£
Car benefit (w)	12,445
Fuel benefit	1,320
Telephone benefit	200
Chauffeur 13,500 x $^9/_{12}$	10,125
Total benefit in kind	£24,090

Working

	£
Maximum value £80,000 x 35%	28,000
Less: $^1/_3$ reduction for mileage	(9,333)
	18,667
Less: $^1/_3$ reduction for age	(6,222)
	£12,445

(6.3.4, 6.3.5)

EMPLOYMENT TAXATION - OTHER MATTERS

The purpose of this session is to:

• outline the workings of the PAYE system

• outline the special system for deduction of tax at source on payments in the construction industry

• describe the main tax implications of share option and incentive schemes for employees

• describe the main features of the profit-related pay system

• explain the extent to which national insurance contributions are payable in respect of employments

References: ICTA 1988 unless otherwise stated.

7.1 The PAYE system

7.1.1 Introduction

The Pay As You Earn method of deducting income tax from salaries and wages applies to all income from offices or employments. Thus PAYE applies not only to weekly wages but also to monthly salaries, annual salaries, bonuses, commissions, directors' fees, pensions and to any other income from an office or employment. PAYE also applies to payments in the form of tradeable assets, tradeable shares or securities or tradeable commodities, vouchers exchangeable for cash or for such items and the use by an employee of a credit token to obtain cash or such items.

It is the employer's duty to deduct income tax from the pay of his employees, whether or not he has been directed to do so by the Revenue. If he fails to do this he may be required to pay over the tax which he should have deducted and, in addition, may be subject to penalties. Officers of the Inland Revenue are empowered by law to inspect employers' records from time to time in order to satisfy themselves that the correct amounts of tax are being deducted and paid over to the Revenue.

7.1.2 How PAYE works

To operate PAYE the employer needs:

(a)   deduction sheets;

(b)   codes for employees which reflect the tax allowances to which the employees are entitled; and

(c)   tax tables.

The amount of tax an employer has to deduct on any pay day is calculated as follows:

(a)   the gross pay due to the employee is determined and added to the total of all previous amounts of gross pay from 6 April to date;

(b)   using the employee's code and Pay Adjustment Tables (Table A), an amount reflecting the effect of the proportion of the employee's allowances from 6 April up to date is ascertained and subtracted from the total pay to date. The balance left is the taxable pay to date;

(c)   the tax due to date is determined by looking up the taxable pay to date in the taxable pay tables (Tables B to D);

(d)   the total tax already paid is deducted from the figure of tax due to date, leaving the tax due to be deducted from the employee's pay on the payday in question.

The PAYE rules require labour, even casual labour, to be made subject to the PAYE system even if the casual worker attends for a single week.

Workers supplied by agencies are to be assessed under Schedule E on their earnings. Entertainers and models are excepted.   s.134

The employer must keep records of each employee's pay and tax and of the total of the employee's and employer's National Insurance contributions and, separately, of the employee's National Insurance contributions at each pay day.

Under the receipts basis the 'date of receipt' for assessability (paragraph 6.1.2) coincides in all material respects with the 'payment date' on which PAYE must be operated.

Employers are required to pay PAYE and NIC deductions made on paydays falling between 6th of a calendar month and 5th of the next calendar month to the Collector within 14 days of the end of the tax month. For example, PAYE deducted on a 26 September 1996 payday must be paid over to the Collector by 19 October 1996.

However, for employers whose monthly payments of PAYE and NIC are less than £600 on average, payments can be made quarterly. Payments for quarters ending 5 July, 5 October, 5 January, and 5 April will be due on the 19th day of those months.

Interest is not charged on late paid monthly or quarterly PAYE and NIC deductions with the exception that it attracts interest - at the rate applying to late paid income tax - from 19 April following the end of the year of assessment in which the deduction was made. There are provisions for paying repayment supplement on the same basis as applies for overpaid income tax if PAYE/NIC has been overpaid.

7.1.3   Anti-avoidance

Payments to employees by way of tradeable assets are also caught within the PAYE net. A tradeable asset is one which is tradeable on an investment, or commodities exchange, or for which 'trading arrangements' exist (ie. the employer arranges for the employee to sell the asset to a third party at a fixed price after payment has been made). The provision extends to vouchers and credit tokens exchangeable for such assets, or for cash.

If a payment is caught, the amount is to be entered onto the deductions working sheet as normal and PAYE calculated thereon. The tax is to be recovered from cash payments made to the employee in that month. Unlike K codes, (see below), there is no 50% limit and the whole of any tax due eg. on the tradeable assets, can be deducted from the cash payments.

The tax must be paid to the Inland Revenue, and to the extent that it is not recovered from the employee, the tax itself becomes a further emolument to be treated as a benefit in kind ie. disclosed on the P11D.

7.1.4 Codes

An employee is normally entitled to various personal tax allowances. Under the PAYE system an amount reflecting the effect of a proportion of these allowances is set against his pay each normal pay day. In order to determine the amount to be set against his pay the allowances are expressed in the form of a code which is used in conjunction with the Pay Adjustment Tables (Table A). The employee is notified of his coding on a Form P2.

Each employee's code is determined by the Revenue and is amended by the Revenue as the employee's circumstances change. The code is normally notified to the employer on a code list or Form P6. The employer is obliged to act on the code notified to him until amended instructions are received from the Revenue, even though the employee may have appealed against the code.

An employee's code may be any one of the following:

(a)   a code of one, two or three numbers followed by the suffix L, H or T; for example 376L;

(b)   the prefix D followed by numbers, for example D40;

(c)   the prefix K followed by numbers, for example K198.

In the case of (a) above the numbers reflect the effect of allowances, but with the last digit omitted. For example, £3,765 becomes 376L (the L refers to the personal allowance). The H suffix indicates an adjustment for the tax reduction given by the married couple's allowance. The code T means that further tax may have to be collected by a year end assessment. Codes which consist of a prefix D followed by a number relate to the higher rate of tax for which tax tables D are provided. These codes should be operated on a non-cumulative basis, ie. each payment is looked at in isolation without reference to any other pay received by the employee since 6 April.

When a code is amended to a code in the D series, no adjustment should be made to the tax previously deducted by reference to the old code. Tax should be deducted from all payments made after the receipt of code D by reference to the corresponding Tax Table D.

When an employee leaves, a certificate on Form P45 (Particulars of employee leaving) must be prepared. This shows the employee's code and details of his income and tax paid to date.

An employee's code may be reduced to reflect anticipated benefits in kind. It may even be negative. Negative codes have prefix K and no suffix. They represent amounts to be added to pay before computing tax, but subject to an overriding rule that no more than 50% of cash pay may be deducted in tax.

7.1.5 End of year procedure

The employer must furnish each employee with a Form P60 showing particulars of the employee's pay and tax deducted in the fiscal year. The deduction sheets must be summarised on a Form P35 which also allows under and over declarations to be dealt with. In addition to these forms, the employer must submit the end of year return (P14), Form P9D (benefits in kind etc. for lower paid employees) and Form P11D (benefits in kind etc. for employees paid £8,500+ p.a. and directors). Forms P9D and P11D are due by 6 June following the end of the tax year. Forms P14 and P35 are due by 19 May after the end of the tax year.

7.1.6 Penalties

Late forms P14 and P35

Penalties can be charged where forms P14 and P35 are submitted late. If forms P14 and P35 not are submitted by 19 May, the penalties which may be imposed are as follows:

(a)   £100 per month of delay per 50 employees (this penalty stops running 12 months after the statutory due date)

(b)   Delay continues more than 12 months after statutory due date: Up to 100% of the tax and Class 1 NIC due but unpaid at the statutory due date

By concession, penalties are not charged provided the Revenue receive the returns within 7 days after the 19 May deadline.

Incorrect forms P14 and P35

A maximum penalty of up to 100% of the tax and Class 1 NIC that would have been underpaid as a result of the error may be imposed.

Late forms P9D and P11D

If the forms are not submitted by the due date of 6 June after the end of the tax year an initial penalty of up to £300 per form may be imposed. If the failure to submit the forms continues after the imposition of the initial penalty, then a further penalty of up to £60 per day per outstanding form can be imposed.

Incorrect forms P9D and P11D

A penalty up to £3,000 per incorrect form can be imposed.

7.1.7 Interest

If PAYE income tax and Class 1 NIC are unpaid by 19 April after the end of the tax year interest is charged from that date.

Class 1A NICs (on cars and fuel) are due by 19 June following the tax year. However, interest only runs from the 19 April after that (eg. 19 April 1997 for 1995/96 contributions).

7.1.8 Charitable donations under payroll deduction scheme

Employees within the PAYE system are able to make tax deductible donations of up to £1,200 pa. to an approved charity of their choice by asking their employer to deduct the donation from their gross earnings *prior* to calculating PAYE. The employer sets up a scheme which requires Revenue approval to be effective and pays the donations to an approved charity, either directly or via an agent. The donations in question must be outright gifts and not payments under deed of covenant.

s.202

To obtain approval, participating employers and their agents must maintain records which must be made available for inspection to the Revenue on request.

7.1.9 PAYE settlement agreements

s.206A

An employer may agree to pay employees' tax liabilities on a range of minor benefits in kind or expenses payments. From 1996/97 this will be done under a PAYE settlement agreement. Items included in such an agreement are exempt from income tax in the hands of the employee and do not have to be declared by either the employer or employee.

7.2 Tax deduction in the construction industry

Subcontractors in the construction industry (the 'lump') have been a headache to the Revenue for many years. Evasion of tax, particularly by labour only subcontractors, is all too easy when remuneration is paid gross. A system, providing for deduction of tax at source on payments within the industry unless the contractor holds an exemption certificate was therefore introduced.

ss.559-567

The scheme applies to payments made by 'contractors' to 'subcontractors' for work involving construction, installation, repairs, fitting, decorating and demolition.

The terms 'contractor' and 'subcontractor' go very much wider than the meanings they normally have in the industry. For example, they extend to local authorities and other public bodies, and to many businesses normally referred to as 'clients'.

The scheme requires action to be taken whenever a contractor pays a subcontractor. Briefly, if the subcontractor holds a subcontractor's tax certificate issued by the Inland Revenue, the contractor pays the subcontractor in full. If, on the other hand, the subcontractor does not hold a certificate the contractor makes a tax deduction from the payment (normally 24%), and passes it over to the Inland Revenue.

Certificates are normally only issued to bona fide businesses in the industry which have a clean tax history going back at least three years starting not more than six years prior to the application. Further conditions include:

(a) a business bank account;

(b) business premises;

(c) the keeping of accounts.

Before paying a subcontractor without deduction, a contractor must satisfy himself that the subcontractor holds a valid certificate. Certificates carry photographs of individual holders.

The payment arrangements, including those where payments average less than £450 per month (see 7.1.2 above), apply as for PAYE collection.

Deductions for a year of assessment, whether monthly or quarterly, attract interest from 19 April following the year end if they remain unpaid. They also qualify for repayment supplement under the usual rules if overpayments of subcontractor deductions are made.

Various changes are to be made to the construction industry tax scheme. These changes will take place from a date to be appointed by the Treasury which will probably be 1 August 1998.

FA 1995 s.139 & Schedule 27

In outline, the main changes will be:

(a) The rate of tax deduction from payments to sub-contractors who do not have an exemption certificate will be determined by the Treasury but will not exceed the basic rate for each year of assessment

(b) All new sub-contractor exemption certificates issued or renewed from January 1995 until the early part of 1998 will show an expiry date of 31 July 1998. This is intended to allow a clean break between the old and new certificates

(c) The present limited exemption certificates allowing tax free payments of up to £150 per week to school leavers and persons in respect of whom a bank guarantee has been given will be abolished

(d)   The definition of a contractor will be extended to include government departments, certain other public bodies, and bodies designated by the Board of Inland Revenue which are carrying out statutory functions. A business outside the construction industry will not have to operate the scheme so long as its average expenditure on construction work does not exceed £1m (previously £250,000).

(e)   The present criminal sanction of a maximum £5,000 fine where a person gives false information, etc. to obtain an exemption certificate, or disposes of or illegally possesses such a certificate, will be replaced by a tax penalty of up to £3,000.

(f)   Exemption certificates will only be issued to individuals, partners and companies which can satisfy the Inland Revenue that they are likely to have an annual business turnover (ie. receipts within the scope of the sub-contractor scheme, excluding the direct cost of materials) equal to or in excess of an amount to be specified in regulations by the Inland Revenue.

(g)   An individual applying for an exemption certificate will no longer have to have worked in the UK for a period of three years. However, in such cases applicants will have to show that they have not been working or have been out of the UK. Where an applicant has been abroad, he will have to satisfy the Inland Revenue that he has complied with the tax laws of the country in which he was resident. There is no change to the current requirement for an applicant to have complied with all his UK tax obligations throughout the period of three years ending with the date of his application.

7.3 Share options and incentives

7.3.1 Introduction

Share schemes are an important element in the remuneration package of key executives. They can provide both a reward for contributions made to the company's success and an incentive to maintain and improve its performance. Because of the attractions of such schemes, the legislation provides for beneficial tax treatment of various types of scheme approved by the Inland Revenue.

Share schemes fall into two main categories: those under which shares are allocated or transferred directly to employees or directors and those which provide for the granting of share options. A share option is a right to buy shares at a price fixed at the time the option is granted. Assuming that the market price of the shares either is or will in the future be above the option price, an employee will then be able to acquire shares at a discount to their full value at the time the option is exercised.

In this section, we consider in outline the tax implications of both unapproved and approved share schemes.

For exam purposes, the Association have said that:

(a)   only the taxation of the employee (ie. not the company) will be examined; and

(b)   questions will not be set on written aspects (ie. presumably questions will be of a computational nature).

7.3.2 Unapproved share option schemes

Where a person is *granted* an option to buy shares, he is not taxed on the grant of the option provided it is exerciseable within seven years of the grant. If the option is exerciseable more than seven years after the grant, a Schedule E benefit arises in the year that the option is granted. The benefit is the market value of the shares at the time that the option is granted less both the cost of the shares under the option and the cost of the option.

s.135

Where a gain is realised on the *exercise* of a share option, the Schedule E benefit is the market value of the shares at the time of the exercise of the option less both the cost of the shares and the cost of the option.

ss.135,136,140

A disposal or release of option rights is treated as an exercise of the rights giving a Schedule E benefit of the excess of the sale proceeds over what was paid for the option.

Any income tax paid on the grant of the option (see above) is deducted from any income tax due on its exercise.

7.3.3 Unapproved share schemes

The normal rules for the taxation of benefits in kind would generally ensure that a gift of shares to an employee or director, as part of his remuneration, would attract a Schedule E liability. Since, however, that liability would be based upon the value of the shares at the time of acquisition, there would, without special provisions, be scope for artificially depressing their value so as to minimise the Schedule E charge. For example, special restrictions could be placed upon the shares given to the employee or director and lifted later so as to restore the shares to their full value.

For a number of years, therefore, anti-avoidance legislation has existed to bring into charge to tax the increase in the value of the shares which takes place when such restrictions are removed. As with much anti-avoidance legislation, the provisions are complex and it is not anticipated that a detailed knowledge would be required at ATT level. Briefly, the present rules provide that an individual who is given shares by reason of his office or employment will suffer a charge to tax if and when, and to the extent that, value is shifted preferentially into the shares concerned. Only individuals within Schedule E Case I (see session 8.2) are subject to these rules. Liability will therefore arise when any rights or restrictions attaching to any shares in the company are varied, and as a result the value of the director's or employee's shareholding is increased.

FA 1988 s.78

7.3.4 Approved share schemes

Introduction

There are three types of approved share scheme of which you need to be aware:

(a)   Profit sharing schemes

(b)   Savings-related share option schemes; and

(c)   "Company" (formerly "executive") share option plans

Of these, (c) is of the greatest practical importance, since these schemes offer a considerable amount of flexibility as to their precise form, and have therefore proved very popular with employers.

Set out below is a summary of the rules applicable to each type of approved scheme and the tax reliefs which are available.

Profit sharing schemes

The Finance Act 1978 introduced legislation designed to encourage companies to set up schemes whereby employees would be able to obtain shares in the company in such a way that no income tax was payable on the receipt of the shares. Capital gains tax may be payable when the shares are sold.

ss.186,187 & Sch 9 & 10

Such a profit sharing scheme must be set up in the form of a trust administered by trustees. The shares falling under the scheme must be held by the trustees for at least *two* years ('the period of retention') before the employee to whom they are allocated can sell his shares. Once the initial two year period of retention is up, employees are free to dispose of shares distributed to them. The scheme must be open to all employees (including part-timers) subject to a qualifying period of up to 5 years employment with the company.

Provided that the employee does not sell the shares for at least *three* years from when they were acquired on his behalf by the trust, there will also be no income tax charge on disposal. If the shares are disposed of before the end of three years then income tax will be payable on the smaller of:

(a)   the original value of the shares; and

(b)   the sale proceeds.

However, where the individual has ceased to be a director or employee of the company or has reached pensionable age, before the disposal, only 50% of the value is charged to tax.

If a disposal does give rise to an income tax assessment the relevant amount is assessable under Schedule E in the year of assessment in which the disposal takes place.

TCGA 1992 s.238

The normal capital gains tax rules apply to all disposals of scheme shares no matter when they take place.

Under a profit sharing scheme there may be annual allocations to the employees. On a subsequent disposal the shares disposed of will be identified on a FIFO basis for the purposes of determining the period of ownership.

The total of the initial market values of the shares allocated to any one participant in a year of assessment must not exceed the greater of £3,000 and 10% of salary (excluding benefits), subject to a ceiling of £8,000.

The term 'profit sharing' is a misnomer as there is no link between the profitability of a company and the value of shares the company chooses to allocate to employees.

Savings related share option schemes

An employer may establish an approved savings-related share option scheme. An employee or director who is granted rights to acquire shares is not charged to income tax on the receipt of that right, nor on the exercise of it. Capital gains tax may be payable, the allowable cost for any disposal being the actual consideration given.

s.185

Such a scheme must be linked to a contractual savings scheme (an SAYE scheme), the repayments of which are used to acquire the shares when the option is exercised. A scheme may not impose a minimum level of contribution higher than £5 per month or permit contributions in excess of £250 per month.

To be approved, the scheme must satisfy a number of conditions. Principal amongst these is the rule that the price at which shares may be acquired must be stated when the option is obtained and must be at least 80% of the market value at that time. There are restrictions on the earliest date on which the option may be exercised (choice of 3, 5 or 7 years) and rules governing various eventualities, such as the death or retirement of the participant, a takeover of the employer company and the inclusion of employees of other companies in the same group.

Sch 9

As with profit sharing schemes, to gain approval, a savings-related share option scheme must be available to virtually all the company's employees, including part timers.

Approved company share option plans

The attractions of approved company share option plans are considerable. Particularly attractive is the lack of a requirement that the scheme must be open to all or nearly all employees. The company can therefore grant these options on a selective basis without penalty, and can include part time employees, but not part time directors. The exercise of the option granted can be made conditional on, for example, achieving a performance target so employees can be positively motivated.

There are no income tax charges on the grant or exercise of the option under a company share option plan, and no charge on the growth in value of the shares. The only charge will be to capital gains tax on the eventual disposal of the shares. There is no minimum time that the employee must hold the shares after exercising his option and before selling the shares, so that the cost of exercising the option can effectively be funded from the sale proceeds. The scheme is not linked to any SAYE scheme, and is much more flexible than the savings-related scheme.

s. 185 & Sch 9

The maximum value of shares any one person can have under option at any time is £30,000.

The options must not be exercisable within 3 years or after 10 years of being granted, and any exercise within 3 years of a previous exercise is not allowed and will be liable to income tax under Schedule E as if the scheme were unapproved.

7.4 Profit related pay

7.4.1 Introduction

Profit-related pay schemes are intended to encourage employees to accept some variability in the level of their pay, reflecting the relative profitability of their employer, by exempting a proportion of their pay which can vary in this way from income tax.

ss.170-184 & Sch 8

7.4.2 Main features of the system

The employment unit

When part of an employee's pay is related to the profit of the 'employment unit' for which he works, within limits, the profit related pay (PRP) is exempt from income tax (but not National Insurance). The amount of PRP eligible for relief may not exceed the lower of £4,000 and 20% of total pay, hence the maximum amount of tax saving for a higher rate tax payer is £1,600 (£4,000 x 40%).

s.171

Excluded employers

Any organisation which has profitable employment units may apply to set up a scheme, other than local or central government.

s.174

Eligible employees

At least 80% of 'eligible employees' must be included in the scheme for it to be approved. Part-time employees (including directors) are included in 'eligible employees'. It is possible to exclude employees with three years' service or less.

Calculation of PRP

The profit pool, which must be paid out entirely as PRP to participating employees, is calculated as a percentage of the profits of the employment unit. The method of determining the profit pool must be specified in the scheme rules.

Mechanics of payment

PRP is treated as income of the tax year in which payment is received.

The employer takes into account the amount of pay which qualifies as PRP when computing taxable pay for PAYE purposes. Although interim PRP payments may be made (eg. based on management accounts), employers have a duty to ensure that they do not pay more than they should without deduction of tax under PAYE. This could happen if the employment unit is profitable for the first part of the year but then suffers a loss. It is the employer, not the employee, who is assessed by the Revenue to recover any under-deduction of tax from pay including interest.

7.5   National insurance contributions (NICs)

7.5.1   Introduction

The Treasury maintains a National Insurance Fund to provide the State retirement pension, unemployment pay, various widow's benefits, invalidity benefit and certain sickness and maternity benefits. These are referred to as "contributory benefits" as they are funded by, and are to some extent calculated by reference to, National Insurance Contributions. At present the Fund runs at a deficit which has to be made up by a Treasury Grant.

Collection is administered by the Contributions Agency under the control of the Department of Social Security (DSS). Most of the actual collection is made by the Inland Revenue either as part of raising Schedule D Case I assessments or through the PAYE system. As roughly £35 billion (£35,000,000,000) flows into the Contributions Agency's coffers each year from taxpayers it is clearly a very important source of revenue.

The non-contributory benefits, such as health care under the NHS, income support, family credit, child benefit, and various disability benefits and the statutory schemes such as those providing sick pay and maternity pay are funded out of general taxation.

There are four main Classes of NIC and they are summarised as follows:

Class 1 is payable in respect of the earnings of employed earners. The employee is liable to primary contributions and the employer to secondary contributions. Class 1A collects NIC from employers in respect of cars and fuel provided to employees.

Class 2 is payable weekly by the self-employed.

Class 3 is paid voluntarily by those not paying Class 1, 2 or 4 in order to preserve their rights to contributory benefits.

Class 4 is paid by the self-employed on their earnings.

In this section we will consider Class 1 and Class 1A. Classes 2 and 4 are dealt with in the Business Income Tax and VAT study text.

7.5.2   Liability to Class 1 contributions

Liability to Class 1 NI contributions arises in relation to 'employed earners'. An employed earner is any person who is gainfully employed in Great Britain, either:

SSCBA 1992
s.2(1)(a)

(a)   under a contract of service; or

(b)   in an office where the emoluments therefrom are chargeable to income tax under Schedule E.

Both a *primary* (employee's) and a *secondary* (employer's) Class 1 contribution is required to be made where the employed earner:

(a)   is aged 16 or over; and

(b)   is paid an amount equal to or greater than the current lower earnings limit (para 7.5.5 below),

unless the employed earner has reached pensionable age (65 for men, 60 for women), in which case a secondary contribution only is required to be paid.

Liability to Class 1 contributions arises in relation to earnings paid - which accords with the Schedule E income tax treatment. Generally, earnings are treated as paid when a sum representing those earnings is placed unreservedly at the disposal of the employee, eg. by credit to his bank account. In the case of a loan made to an employee in anticipation of earnings, no Class 1 liability arises unless and until the employee is released from his obligation to repay the loan. This does not apply in the case of a director: NI contributions are required to be made at the time when the director has an unfettered right to draw on sums put at his disposal unless the director's account which is overdrawn is to be settled by monies other than remuneration eg. dividends.

7.5.3 Primary contributions

Employed earners below pensionable age, whose earnings in the 'earnings period' (para 7.5.6 below) exceed the lower limit, are required to pay 10% of their earnings as a primary contribution. Only a 2% rate applies on earnings up to the lower limit. In addition an upper earnings limit applies: no contribution is required in respect of earnings in excess of that limit.

Broadly, earnings comprise gross pay, excluding payments in kind which cannot be turned into cash by surrender eg. company car, holidays, and also excluding tips received directly from customers. In computing earnings, no deduction is made for superannuation contributions or for charitable gifts under an approved payroll giving scheme. However, an *employer's* contribution to the employee's approved personal pension is excluded from earnings.

Earnings include payments in shares (apart from shares in the employer), units in unit trusts, loan stock, tradeable assets (defined as for PAYE), assets which can be traded on a UK investment or commodities exchange, and also gemstones and 'fine wines'.

You should note that genuine business expenses met directly, or reimbursed by the employer, are not treated as earnings. For example, if an employee uses his own car and is reimbursed a business mileage allowance the 'earnings' element is restricted to the excess over the FPCS rates (applying for Schedule E) using the under 4,000 miles scale regardless of actual mileage. Exemption also applies to personal incidental expenses if exempt Schedule E as de minimis - ie. within £5 per night.

As a rule of thumb, if an item is not chargeable to tax under Schedule E there is unlikely to be an NIC charge - with the notable exception of profit related pay. If an employer pays all or part of an employee's council tax on accommodation provided by reason of the employment, the payment counts as earnings unless the accommodation is exempted from an income tax charge as job-related.

Note that where the employer pays a bill on behalf of the employee where the employee contracted for the supply of the goods or services (ie. the employee's name is on the invoice), this amount is included in earnings.

7.5.4 Secondary contributions

The employer is required to pay secondary contributions in accordance with a graduated scale of rates. Note that no upper earnings limit applies to the employer's contribution.

The secondary contribution is an allowable expense in computing the employer's Schedule D Case I profits.

7.5.5 Rates of Class 1 contributions

Rates for Class 1 contributions for an employee are shown on page (ix).

Rates for Class 1 weekly contributions for an employer are:

Below £61 per week	nil
£61.00 to £109.99 per week	3%
£110.00 to £154.99 per week	5%
£155.00 to £209.99 per week	7%
£210.00 or more per week	10.2%

The rate for the employer applies to all the earnings (eg. for weekly earnings of £195 secondary NIC is 7% x £195)

Both these rates apply where the employee is not contracted out of SERPS - the state earnings-related pension scheme. SERPS provides for the basic retirement pension, widow's pension, widowed mother's allowance and invalidity pension to be augmented by an amount related to the level of the contributor's earnings. The employer may prefer to make his own arrangements for the provision of earnings-related pensions for his employees through a private occupational scheme. In that case, the employees are contracted out of SERPS, provided the scheme meets certain statutory requirements. It is also possible for an employee to use a personal pension scheme to contract out. This topic is not discussed further as the Association have listed it as an exclusion.

7.5.6 Earnings periods

An earnings period is a period to which earnings paid to an employed earner are deemed to relate and by reference to which the liability to Class 1 contributions is assessed. The period in respect of which the earnings in question are earned is irrelevant.

Where earnings are paid at regular intervals, the earnings period will generally be equated with the payment interval, eg. one week or one month. This is subject to the proviso that an earnings period must be at least seven days in length. The first earnings period in any tax year always begins on the first day of that tax year.

Example

> Angela is paid weekly and Betty is paid monthly, therefore their earnings periods for NI purposes are weekly and monthly respectively.
>
> Angela is paid £75 on 15 April 1996. The first weekly earnings period for 1996/97 runs from 6 April to 12 April 1996 and the second from 13 April to 19 April 1996. Therefore the payment on 15 April 1996 is assessed to NI in the second earnings period of 1996/97.
>
> Betty is paid £320 on 30 April 1996. This falls within the first monthly earnings period of 1996/97 which runs from 6 April 1996 to 5 May 1996.

Note that in the case of regular monthly or weekly earnings periods, the end of those periods coincides with the end of the tax week or tax month of the PAYE system.

Where an employee has a weekly earnings period, there will be a short earnings period (ie. less than seven days) at the end of each tax year. This will comprise one day (normal years) or two days (leap years), but never more than two days. This is an exception to the rule that an earnings period must be at least seven days in length.

If an employee has two or more regular pay patterns (eg. monthly salary plus half-yearly bonus), the shortest pay interval will form the earnings period, unless this rule is used as a means of avoiding contributions. In that case the longest interval determines the earnings period.

Example

Colin is a salesman, receiving a monthly salary, half-yearly commission and an annual bonus.

He receives the following amounts:

15/6/96:	commission for half-year to 31 March 1996	£2,000
18/6/96:	annual bonus: y/e 31 March 1996	£1,800
30/6/96:	monthly salary June 1996	£1,250

The earnings period is monthly and therefore all of the amounts above fall within the same earnings period, 6 June 1996 to 5 July 1996. Primary and secondary contributions for that month (PAYE month 3) will be based on earnings of £5,050 (£2,000 + 1,800 + 1,250).

As Colin has a monthly earnings period, his earnings will be compared to monthly, rather than weekly limits.

Special rules apply to determine the earnings period where there is no regular pay interval.

Special rules also apply in the case of company directors, regardless of whether they are paid at regular intervals or not. Briefly, where a person is a director at the commencement of the tax year, his earnings period is the tax year, even if he ceases to be director during the year. In the case where a person is first appointed as a director during a tax year, the earnings period is the number of tax weeks from the week in which he is appointed to the end of the tax year.

Example

Freddie is first appointed as a director of Maypole Ltd on 4 June 1996. 4 June 1996 falls into the tax week commencing 2 June 1996 and the number of tax weeks to 5 April 1997 is 45. Freddie's earnings period is therefore 45 weeks. His NIC position as an employee prior to his appointment is not affected by this rule.

Note that there are 53 'tax weeks' in a tax year, irrespective of the fact that the 53rd tax week contains only one or two days.

7.5.7 Class 1A NIC

Employers are liable for Class 1A contributions where they provide cars for the private use of their employees and where private use fuel is also provided for use in an employer's car. The contributions are 10.2% of the taxable benefits for Schedule E purposes.

s.10 SSCBA 1992

Payments are collected annually in arrears. The 1996/97 Class 1A contributions are to be included with the PAYE and NIC payment for the month ending 5 June 1997.

Employees are exempted from primary contributions on the use of the car and on fuel where it is used in an employer's car. The Class 1A rules only apply to employers.

No liability arises if the employee earns less than £8,500 pa. or if the car is not available for private use or if the employee fully reimburses the cost of private motoring.

QUESTIONS

1. What is the function of a PAYE code?

2. What is a form P11D used for?

3. For the week ending Friday 19 January 1997 five employees of an engineering company earn gross pay as follows:

	£
Alan	53.00
Betty	64.00
Carl	180.00
Darren	240.00
Eleanor	480.00

    Show the primary and secondary contributions payable assuming none are contracted out and all are below pensionable age.

4. Shifty Sales Ltd provides three of its employees (all earning over £8,500 pa) with company cars (all under 4 years old) for 1996/97 as follows:

Employee	cc	Cost (new)	Business miles
Stuart	1,000	£7,500	6,000
Terry	2,000	£11,800	15,000
Una	3,500	£23,400	2,000

    All fuel (petrol) is paid for by the company. Stuart reimburses the company for all of his private mileage but Terry and Una pay only £50 each a month.

    You are required to show the Class 1A NIC that is payable for 1996/97.

5. Norman joined Grange Ltd, a 'leading edge' clothes fashion retailer, as a director on 18 June 1996. He is paid a basic salary of £600 pm. at the end of each month (£300 in June) and is paid a bonus on the basis of half yearly sales. His January 1997 remuneration included a bonus of £18,000.

    You are required to compute the amount of primary Class 1 NIC payable on the January remuneration assuming the exact percentage method applies. (This pro rates the earnings limits to the director's annual earnings period and computes liability on a cumulative basis).

SOLUTIONS

1.   It enables the employer to determine how much tax-free pay an employee is entitled to on each pay day (7.1.4).

2.   The form P11D is used by employers to report to the Inland Revenue expense payments and benefits received by employees paid £8,500+ p.a. and directors (7.1.5).

3.   Alan   no liability as below £61 pw

Betty	- Primary	(£61 x 2%) + (£3 x 10%)	=	£1.52
	- Secondary	£64 x 3%	=	£1.92
Carl	- Primary	(£61 x 2%) + (£119 x 10%)	=	£13.12
	- Secondary	£180 x 7%	=	£12.60
Darren	- Primary	(£61 x 2%) + (£179 x 10%)	=	£19.12
	- Secondary	£240 x 10.2%	=	£24.48
Eleanor	- Primary	(£61 x 2%) + (£394 x 10%)	=	£40.62 (max)
	- Secondary	£480 x 10.2%	=	£48.96

4.

Stuart:	Car	(£7,500 x 35%= £2,625 less 1/3 (875)= 1,750 x 10.2%)	178.50
	Fuel	(none - all private petrol reimbursed)	-
Terry:	Car	(£11,800 x 35% = £4,130 less 1/3 (1,377) = 2,753 x 10.2%)	280.81
	Fuel	(890 x 10.2%)	90.78
Una:	Car	(£23,400 x 35% = 8,190 x 10.2%)	835.38
	Fuel	(1,320 x 10.2%)	134.64
		Total Class 1A	£1,520.11

5.   Norman (director) - Earnings period remaining in 1996/97 (18.6.96 - 5.4.97) is 43 weeks.

	£
Lower earnings limit £61 x 43	2,623
Upper earnings limit £455 x 43	19,565
Cumulative pay to December: £300 + (6 x £600)	£3,900

Clearly the 2% band is used and until £19,565 is exceeded any further pay is liable to primary contributions at 10%.

January pay at £18,600 (and £3,900 to date) exceeds the cumulative UEL of £19,565.

NIC liability for January limited to:

19,565 - 3,900 = 15,665 @ 10% = £1,566.50

The purpose of this session is to:

- define the terms residence, ordinary residence and domicile and explain their significance

- describe the three cases of Schedule E and the circumstances in which each applies

- outline the rules of the special deduction for Schedule E Case I taxpayers who work abroad for 365 days or more

- outline the scope and basis of assessment of Schedule D Cases IV and V

References: ICTA 1988 unless otherwise stated.

8.1 Residence, ordinary residence and domicile

8.1.1 Introduction

In Session 1 of this study text we explained that a taxpayer's *residence, ordinary residence* and *domicile* had important consequences in establishing the treatment of his UK and overseas income. The rules are now set out in detail.

8.1.2 Residence and ordinary residence

General principles

A person is deemed to be resident in the UK for a given tax year if, in that tax year, he is present in the UK for a total of 183 days or more (days of arrival and departure are normally excluded). There are no exceptions to this.

ss.334-336

IR 20 (1993)
para 1.2

It is possible to be regarded as UK resident for a tax year even if the individual spends less than 183 days in the UK:

(a)   Individuals leaving the UK for short periods remain UK resident if they usually live in the UK. Non-residence would generally only be achieved by complete absence from the UK for the tax year.

(b)   Individuals leaving the UK permanently are treated as remaining UK resident if visits to the UK average 91 days or more pa.

(c)   Visitors to the UK are treated as UK resident for a tax year if visits are regular and after four tax years visits have averaged 91 days or more pa. Residence applies for the fifth year onwards. However, a visitor to the UK is treated as UK resident from the start of the first tax year if it is clear from the outset that the 91 days average of visits to the UK is intended.

(d)   Short term visitors coming for a period of at least two years employment in the UK are treated as UK resident from the day of arrival to the day of departure.

For the purpose of the 91 day test above, days which are spent in the UK because of exceptional circumstances beyond the individual's control (eg. illness) are excluded from the calculation.

SP2/91

A person who is resident in the UK will be deemed to be ordinarily resident where his residence is of an habitual nature. Ordinary residence implies a greater degree of permanence than mere residence. A person, being deemed by the Inland Revenue to be ordinarily resident, may appeal to the Special Commissioners within three months of the inspector's decision. The significance of ordinary residence is principally in connection with Schedule D Cases IV and V (see section 8.3), interest on some government securities and bank deposit interest.

Strictly, each tax year must be looked at as a whole: a person is resident and/or ordinarily resident for either no part, or all, of the tax year, depending on the circumstances. Thus a person who is ordinarily resident in the UK and who goes abroad for a period which does not include a complete tax year, is regarded as remaining resident and ordinarily resident in the UK throughout. It is the practice by concession, however, to split the tax year if the person:

ESC A11

(a)   is a new permanent resident or comes to stay for at least three years, provided he was previously not ordinarily resident; or

(b)   has left the UK for permanent residence abroad, provided that he becomes not ordinarily resident in the UK; or

(c)   comes to the UK to take up employment for a period which is expected to be at least two years. Again, the concessionary treatment is available only to an individual who was not ordinarily resident in the UK prior to his arrival; or

(d)   is proceeding abroad to take up employment which covers at least a whole tax year: see below.

A wife's residence and ordinary residence is quite independent of her husband's status and is determined by her own circumstances. If for example, a husband is employed abroad full-time, and his wife goes out to join him but later returns to the UK without having been away for a complete tax year, she is regarded as remaining resident and ordinarily resident here although he may be not resident and not ordinarily resident. There is, however, a concession which can benefit a spouse accompanying a person taking up full time employment abroad which can over ride this principle of independent status (see below).

The Revenue will generally decide whether an individual is full-time employed on the basis of the particular circumstances of his employment and are not prepared to issue blanket guidelines.

Leaving the UK

As explained above, a person who has been resident or ordinarily resident in the UK is treated as remaining resident if he goes abroad for short periods (possibly less than one year) only.

In 1960 the taxpayer founded a band known as the Dave Clark Five which disbanded in 1970. From that date Mr Clark's activity was promoting the band's catalogue. In December 1977 Polydor paid Mr Clark a large sum for the copyright of some of the band's songs. To reduce his tax liability on this sum, Mr Clark extended his proposed visit to the USA to exceed a whole tax year. He remained in the USA from 3 April 1978 to 2 May 1979. S.334 ICTA 1988 provides that a British subject who has been ordinarily resident in the UK continues to be subject to income tax notwithstanding that he may have left the UK if he has so left for the purposes only of occasional residence abroad.

Reed v Clark
(1985)

The courts held that a year abroad was a sufficiently long enough period to not be occasional residence abroad. Mr Clark was not UK resident or ordinarily resident for 1978/79 and therefore not liable to tax on the sum, because of the preceding year basis of assessment.

If a person claims that he has ceased to be resident and ordinarily resident in the UK and can produce some evidence for this, such as selling his UK home and setting up a permanent home abroad, then his claim is normally provisionally admitted from the day of his departure. If no such evidence can be produced the decision will be postponed for three years and then retrospective adjustments made accordingly.

If a person goes abroad for full-time service under a contract of employment and:

ESC A11

(a)   his absence from the UK is for a period which includes a complete tax year; and

(b)   interim visits to the UK do not amount to six months or more in any one tax year or three months or more on average,

he is normally regarded as not resident and not ordinarily resident for the whole period of the contract, even if this means splitting tax years.

There is a similar concessionary treatment for the accompanying (or visiting) spouse of such an individual if she (or he) also satisfies conditions (a) and (b) above. In the year of departure and year of return the accompanying spouse's residence status will be dealt with on a split year basis.

Coming to the UK

A person whose home has previously been abroad and who comes to the UK to take up permanent residence here is regarded as resident and ordinarily resident from the date of his arrival.

A person who comes to the UK to work for a period of at least two years is treated as resident here for the whole period from arrival to departure. If he does not initially intend to stay for at least three years and does not buy accommodation or take a lease exceeding three years on accommodation, he is treated as becoming ordinarily resident from the start of the tax year following the third anniversary of his arrival. This rule applies whether the individual comes for employment in the UK or for some other purpose.

SP 17/91

If an individual comes to the UK and, before the point at which the above rule would impose ordinary residence, he either buys or takes a greater than three year lease on accommodation, or changes his intention on the length of his stay in the UK, he will become ordinarily resident:

(a)   from the date of first arrival if the relevant event occurs in his first tax year in the UK; or

(b)   from the start of the tax year in which the event occurs.

For example, if Hans arrived in the UK on 1 October 1994 intending only to stay for 30 months, he will become ordinarily resident in 1998/99 if he still remains in the UK by then. If he bought a house in the UK in December 1994 he would be ordinarily resident for 1994/95 (from 1 October 1994). However, if he delayed buying a house until July 1997 he would not become ordinarily resident until 1997/98.

8.1.3 Domicile

Broadly speaking, a person is domiciled in the country in which he has his permanent home. Domicile is distinct from nationality or residence. A person may be resident in more than one country, but at any given time he can only be domiciled in one. A person acquires a domicile of origin at birth; this is normally the domicile of his father and therefore not necessarily the country where he himself was born. A person retains this domicile until he acquires a different *domicile of choice*. A domicile of choice can be acquired only by individuals aged 16 or over.

If, before reaching that age, the person (eg. father) whose domicile determined the minor's own domicile, acquires a new domicile of choice, the minor's domicile changes similarly - *domicile of dependency*.

To acquire a domicile of choice a person must sever his ties with the country of his domicile of origin and settle in another country with the clear intention of making his permanent home there. Long residence in another country is not in itself enough to prove that a person has acquired a domicile of choice there unless it can be regarded as indicating intention; there has to be evidence that he firmly intends to live there permanently.

Re Clore (dec'd) (1984)

8.1.4 The rules applied

Generally, a UK resident is liable to UK income tax on his UK and foreign income whereas a non-resident is liable to UK income tax only on income arising in the UK. UK residents enjoy personal allowances. Non-residents do not, except that citizens of the Commonwealth or of the European Economic Area are entitled to claim allowances - see para 2.4.4.

A UK resident who is not domiciled in the UK is liable to UK tax on foreign income on a *remittance basis* only - ie. only to the extent that such income is brought to the UK, except for income assessed under Schedule E Case I (see below). The remittance basis for foreign income also applies to British subjects resident but not ordinarily resident in the UK.

Interest on most UK government securities is exempt from UK income tax if the recipient is not ordinarily resident in the UK. The securities include $3^{1}/_{2}$% War Loan, all issues of Funding Loan and most issues of Treasury Stock and Exchequer Loan. By extra statutory concession, UK bank deposit and building society interest is treated in a similar manner.

s.47

ESC B13

8.2 The case system of Schedule E

8.2.1 Three cases of Schedule E

For the purposes of earnings from an office or employment (the meaning of which was considered in Session 6), Schedule E is divided into three Cases. The Case under which a taxpayer may be assessed is determined largely by reference to the taxpayer's residence status and the place where he performs his duties, as indicated in the following table:

s.19(1)

Status	Duties wholly or partly in UK		Duties wholly outside the UK
	Emoluments for UK duties	Emoluments for non UK duties	
Resident and ordinarily resident	I	I	I*
Resident but not ordinarily resident	II	III	III
Not resident	II	Not taxable	Not taxable

*Case III for foreign emoluments. Foreign emoluments are emoluments earned by a *non-domiciled* individual employed by a *non-resident employer*.

8.2.2 Receipts and remittance basis

If a taxpayer is assessed under Schedule E Case I or II, then the assessment will be computed by reference to emoluments *received* during the year of assessment. If, on the other hand, he is assessed under Case III the assessment will take into account only amounts actually *remitted* to the UK from abroad. Thus Case III earnings received abroad but not remitted to the UK are effectively exempt from UK tax.

s.19(1)

8.2.3 The 365-day rule

For individuals who receive emoluments under Schedule E Case I and who are resident and ordinarily resident in the UK, there is a special relief (known as the '365-day' rule) if they are required to work abroad for a year or more.

s.193, Sch 12

When considering the case of someone leaving the UK to work abroad there are two *quite separate* approaches:

(a)   if the job fits the description of a *contract of employment* and the absence from the UK includes a complete year of assessment, then the taxpayer becomes non-resident and not ordinarily resident for the period of the contract (see 8.1.2). Clearly, there can then be no question of UK tax on the overseas income. But if the taxpayer has UK income, he may set his UK personal allowances against it by virtue of s.278;

(b)   if the above does not apply and the individual remains resident in the UK (and therefore entitled to UK personal allowances) there is nevertheless an important concession under Schedule E Case I. A taxpayer who works abroad for a *'continuous period'* of 365 days or more, *not* necessarily encompassing a tax year (a *qualifying period*) enjoys a deduction of 100%, ie. the Schedule E income is free of UK tax. An earnings basis applies to determine the emoluments relieved. Thus payments received after the qualifying period are still relieved if they were earned abroad.

The 100% deduction applies to earnings net of allowable deductions such as pension contributions and expenses. Thus if the qualifying period only covers part of a tax year it is not possible to set a whole year's deductions against just the part of the year's earnings not covered by the 100% relief.

A period abroad will be treated as continuous unless during that period the taxpayer is in the UK for either:

(a)   more than 62 continuous days. The day of arrival is included, but not the day of departure, as the location of the taxpayer at the end of a day determines his location for the whole of that day. This is known as the 'midnight' rule; or

(b)   any period which together with previous UK visits exceeds 1/6 of the qualifying total to date. This means that an absence abroad ceases to be a qualifying period if, after any period abroad, the cumulative total of UK visits exceeds 1/6 of the total to date.

Example

Mr X Patriot had the following itinerary in the calendar years 1995 and 1996:

Left the UK on 1 Sept 1995	Returned to the UK on 1 Oct 1995
Left the UK on 21 Oct 1995	Returned to the UK on 9 Apr 1996
Left the UK on 19 May 1996	Returned to the UK on 6 Sept 1996
Left the UK on 11 Oct 1996	Returned to the UK on 20 Dec 1996

Mr Patriot's emoluments for 1995/96 were £25,000 and for 1996/97 were £28,000, and his employment covered the whole of both years.

You are required to state what his Schedule E Case I assessments will be for each of those years.

Solution

The easiest approach is to try and build up a 'sandwich' of absences and presences. We start with the first two absences:

		Absence (days)	Presence (days)
(A)	1.9.95 - 30.9.95 (inc.)	30	
(P)	1.10.95 - 20.10.95 (inc.)		20
(A)	21.10.95 - 8.4.96 (inc)	171	
		201	20

As the 'sandwich' is built up, the tests mentioned above are applied *every time the taxpayer returns to the country*.

So we test, first of all, on 1.10.95. Clearly the period of absence between 1.9.95 and 30.9.95 is continuous and so we can move on.

The test is next to be applied on 9.4.96. On that date:

(1)   the most recent period of presence is less than 63 continuous days; *and*

(2)   the cumulative total of presences so far is less than one sixth of the total tour to date (ie. 201 + 20 days).

Since *both* these tests are passed, we have a deemed continuous period of absence between 1.9.95 and 8.4.96. We can continue building up the sandwich:

		Absence (days)	Presence (days)
	B/f	201	20
(P)	9.4.96 - 18.5.96 (inc.)		40
(A)	19.5.96 - 5.9.96 (inc.)	110	
		311	60

We test this time on 6.9.96. On that date:

(a)   the most recent period of presence is less than 63 continuous days; *and*

(b)   the cumulative total of presences (60 days) is less than one sixth of the total tour to date (ie. 311 + 60 days).

Since both tests are passed there is a deemed continuous period of absence of 371 days between 1.9.95 and 5.9.96.

There is one final absence to deal with:

		Absence (days)	Presence (days)
	B/f	311	60
(P)	6.9.96 - 10.10.96 (inc.)		35
(A)	11.10.96 - 19.12.96 (inc.)	70	
		381	95

We test on 20.12.96 and find that the cumulative total of presences (95 days) is *greater* than one sixth of the total tour to date (381 + 95 days). Continuity has thus been broken by the taxpayer's presence in the UK between 6.9.96 and 10.10.96.

The continuous period of absence, therefore, extends only from 1.9.95 to 5.9.96 (inclusive).

The 371 days of this period of absence fall into two different tax years:

1995/96	218 days
1996/97	153 days

The assessments for each of those years are as follows:

	1995/96 £
Emoluments	25,000
Less: $\frac{218}{366}$ x £25,000	(14,891)
Schedule E Case I	£10,109

	1996/97 £
Emoluments	28,000
Less: $\frac{153}{365}$ x £28,000	(11,737)
Schedule E Case I	£16,263

Where the taxpayer is a seafarer (ie. employed on a ship) the maximum stay in the UK is 183 days (rather than 62) and the maximum UK fraction of the absence abroad is one half (rather than one sixth).

Sch 12 para 3(2A)

8.2.4   Travelling expenses for work abroad

As we have already seen, the cost of travelling to the site at which the duties of an employment are to be performed is not normally a deductible expense under the restrictive s.198 rule. However, there are a number of special provisions granting relief where foreign travel is involved. We consider first the position of UK employees going to work abroad. In para 8.2.5 below, the rules applicable to foreign nationals coming to work in the UK are outlined.

An individual who is resident and ordinarily resident in the UK (and taxed under Case I of Schedule E) is entitled to deduct, under s.198, the cost of travelling to an overseas location where the duties of the employment are to be performed. A deduction is also given for the cost of return travel to the UK upon completion of the overseas duties. In a case where the duties of the employment are to be performed *wholly* outside the UK, the relief is restricted to those *not* in receipt of foreign emoluments (defined, as you will recall, as emoluments received by a non-UK domiciled employee from a non-UK resident employer). s.193(2) & (3)
s.194(1),(3)-(6)

Where board and lodging is provided at the overseas location, the expenses so incurred are similarly deductible. This applies, regardless of whether the cost is met directly by the employer or incurred initially by the employee and reimbursed by the employer. s.193(4)

Relief is extended to the cost of certain journeys by the employee's spouse and any minor (aged under 18) children, but only where the employee's period of absence from the UK is at least 60 continuous days. In that case, relief is available for the cost of the return journey, where the spouse and/or children accompany the employee when he first leaves the UK. Alternatively, if the spouse and/or children visit the employee during his time abroad, the cost of up to two outward and return journeys in a tax year is eligible for relief. This relief does *not* extend to other costs incurred in connection with the visit eg. additional accommodation. s.194(1)&(2)

8.2.5 Travelling expenses of employees coming to the UK

Special relief for travelling expenses is available to individuals who are not domiciled in the UK but who come to the UK to carry out the duties of their office or employment. s.195

Provided various conditions are met (see below), the relief mirrors quite closely that available to UK nationals going abroad, described in para 8.2.4 above. That is, the expenses which are deductible from the Schedule E Case I or II emoluments received for the UK duties comprise:

(a)   the cost of travelling from the employee's usual home overseas to the UK and returning home at the end of his UK duties; and

(b)   where the employee remains in the UK for at least 60 continuous days, the cost of return journeys by his spouse and minor children, either accompanying him on his arrival or visiting him subsequently. As before, visits are limited to two in any one tax year.

Some restrictions need to be considered. Firstly, relief is only available if one of two conditions is met on the date the employee arrives in the UK. On that date, the employee must either:

(a)   not have been resident in the UK in either of the two years of assessment preceding that in which the date of arrival falls; or

(b)   not have been physically present in the UK at any time during the two years immediately before the date of arrival.

Secondly, assuming either condition (a) or condition (b) is met, relief is available only for expenses incurred during a five year period, commencing with the date of arrival in the UK.

If a non-domiciled employee's removal expenses are reimbursed by his employer, up to £8,000 will be excluded from being assessed as a Sch E benefit (see 6.4 above).

8.2.6 Termination payments after foreign service

Payments received on termination of an employment which included an element of foreign service may be exempt from tax. Complete exemption is given where the foreign service element is "very substantial".

For the purposes of this exemption, the employee's period of service is treated as including a very substantial element of foreign service, where the foreign service comprises:

s.188(3)

(a)   three-quarters of the whole period of service; or

(b)   the last 10 years, where the whole period of service is in excess of 10 years; or

(c)   half of the total period of service, including any ten out of the last 20 years, where the total period of service is in excess of 20 years.

Accordingly, payments on termination of an employment falling within the conditions of either (a), (b) or (c) above are entirely exempt from tax.

Foreign service is service, the emoluments of which are not chargeable under Case I of Schedule E, and includes emoluments which attract the 100% deduction described in para 8.2.3 above, due to the recipient having spent a continuous period of at least 365 days abroad.

Sch 11, para 10

Example

Matthew, Mark and Luke each receive a termination payment of £50,000 from their former employer, Getrich Enterprises Ltd. The following details are relevant:

Matthew: employed by the company for six years, of which five were spent in foreign service;

Mark: employed by the company for 13 years. For the first 10 years, Mark was engaged in foreign service. The last three years were spent in the UK;

Luke: employed by the company for 30 years, the pattern of his employment being:

Years 1 - 5   Foreign service

Years 6 - 11   UK service

Years 12 - 25   Foreign service

Years 26 - 30   UK service

You are required to state whether these termination payments are exempt from UK tax and, if so, on what grounds.

Solution

Each of these employments includes a substantial element of foreign service and the termination payments are therefore exempt from UK income tax.

Matthew: Foreign service represents 83% (5/6) of the total period of service. Therefore condition (a) above is satisfied.

Mark: condition (b) above is *not* satisfied because three of the last 10 years were spent in the UK. However, foreign service comprises more than 75% of the total period of employment (10/13 = 77%), therefore condition (a) is satisfied.

Luke: neither condition (a) nor condition (b) is satisfied. However, foreign service comprises more than 50% of the total period (19/30 = 63%) and more than 10 out of the last 20 years, therefore the payment is exempt under condition (c) above.

After all other exemptions, if part of the termination payment is still taxable and there has been foreign service during the period of employment, a fraction of the otherwise taxable payment may be deducted equal to:

Sch 11, para 3 & 14

$$\frac{\text{period of foreign service}}{\text{total length of service up to the relevant date}}$$

8.3   Schedule D Cases IV and V

8.3.1   Scope of charge

The basis of assessment for Cases IV and V is identical and so the distinction between them is not important. However:

(a)   Case IV deals with income from *securities* outside the UK and includes: s.18(3)

    (i)   securities of foreign governments;

    (ii)   debentures and secured loan stock in foreign companies; and

    (iii) foreign mortgage loans;

(b)   Case V deals with income from *possessions* outside the UK including: s.18(3)

    (i)   rent from property abroad (see 4.1.10);

    (ii)   dividends from overseas companies;

    (iii) partnership profits from a business carried on and controlled wholly outside the UK; and

    (iv)   foreign pensions.

If, however, dividends from foreign companies or other forms of foreign investment income are paid through a UK paying agent who acts as a custodian of the shares or securities (eg. a bank) then Case IV or V does not apply. The paying agent must deduct tax at the lower rate and the taxed income is dealt with on an actual basis in the hands of the shareholder, to determine the extent of any higher rate tax liability.

UK tax deduction does not apply where the UK paying agent merely arranges to clear the cheque for the foreign dividend or interest.

Similarly, the charge to income tax on foreign source investment income (which has not passed through a UK paying agent with custodian status and is therefore not accompanied by a UK tax credit) follows the same rules applicable to UK savings income. Thus UK or foreign interest or dividends falling within the basic rate band is taxable at 20%.

Any foreign tax paid on foreign source income is allowed as a credit up to the amount of the UK tax due on that income. The foreign income is treated as the top slice of the taxpayer's income for this purpose.

8.3.2   Basis of assessment

The basis period rules for Cases IV and V are the same as for Case I/II if the income is from a trade etc, or otherwise as for Case III, including the opening and closing year rules for old sources and the distinction between old (pre-6 April 1994) and new sources.   ss.65 - 67

The remittance basis (ie. only such income as is brought to the UK is taxed) applies to:

(a)   persons not *domiciled* in the UK; and

(b)   British subjects not *ordinarily resident* in the UK.

When the remittance basis applies, income is treated as first arising when it is first remitted to the UK. This may determine whether the income is from an old source or a new source.

The terms 'resident', 'ordinarily resident' and 'domiciled' were explained above.

If the remittance basis applies dividends or interest falling within the basic rate band are taxed at 24% instead of 20%.

For persons taxed on the arising basis, annuities and pensions from a foreign earned source are taxed only to the extent of 90% of the amount arising.

QUESTIONS

1. Meredith is domiciled in the state of New York, but resident and ordinarily resident in the UK. To what extent is Meredith charged to UK income tax on rental income from letting a property in New York?

2. Under which case of Schedule E are the following individuals assessed?

   (a) John, resident and ordinarily resident in the UK but domiciled in Australia, performing duties wholly in the UK for an Australian company.

   (b) Alberto, neither resident nor ordinarily resident in the UK and domiciled in Italy, who performs duties in the UK for a UK company.

   (c) Henry, resident, ordinarily resident and domiciled in the UK, performing duties partly in the UK and partly in Germany.

3. Stefan is resident and ordinarily resident in the UK but domiciled in Norway. He works for a French company, the duties of the employment being carried out wholly in France. To what extent is Stefan charged to UK income tax on his salary from his French employer?

4. Martin is on the 8am flight from London Heathrow to Paris Charles de Gaulle on 8 October 1996. He returns to the UK on 20 December 1996, landing at Heathrow at 11.30pm.

   How long (in days) is his period of absence from the UK?

5. Hector, who is resident, ordinarily resident and domiciled in the UK, receives a pension of £8,000 per annum from his former employer, a Canadian company based in Montreal. Hector used to work in Montreal.

   Under what Schedule and Case and to what extent is Hector charged to UK income tax on the pension?

SOLUTIONS

1.   Only to the extent that such income is remitted to the UK (8.1.4).

2.   (a)   Case I

        (b)   Case II

        (c)   Case I (with a possible 100% deduction for emoluments for the non-
              UK duties).

        (8.2.1)

3.   On a remittance basis, under Schedule E Case III (8.2.2).

4.   8 October - 19 December 1996 inclusive (applying the "midnight rule") ie.
        73 days (8.2.3).

5.   Under Schedule D Case V on the arising basis, but on only 90% (ie. £7,200)
        of the full amount (8.3.1 and 8.3.2).

Illustrative questions and suggested solutions

QUESTIONS

1.   MRS BUTCHER

Mrs Butcher, a widow (since 1985), is aged 67. Her income in the years ended 5 April 1996 and 1997 consisted of:

	1996 £	1997 £
State retirement pension	3,060	3,180
Occupational pension (PAYE £980; £1,133)	4,700	4,900
Building society interest received (net)	3,525	4,000
Rent from let cottage, (unfurnished) net of allowable expenses	240	977
Interest on 3½% War Loan	355	355
Interest from National Savings Bank ordinary account (opened 1985)	100	120
Dividends received from UK companies	150	240
Purchased life annuity including agreed capital element £2,120 (gross)	2,500	2,500

Mrs Butcher's grandchildren, Bill (aged 19 and still at school trying his GCSEs again) and Jane (aged 13) live with Mrs Butcher and have been maintained by her since the children's parents disappeared in Sicily 5 years ago.

You are required to calculate Mrs Butcher's income tax repayment for 1996/97, assuming that no tax has been paid by direct assessment.

2.   ALBERT

Albert owns a lock-up shop which he let for some years to Jim at a full rent of £2,400 per annum payable on the first of each month in advance. The tenancy terminated on 30 June 1996 and the premises remained vacant until 29 September 1996.

On 29 September 1996 Albert granted a lease of the shop to Jean (a trader) for a term of 11 years at a full rent of £1,600 per annum payable on the usual quarter days in advance. In consideration of the granting of the lease Albert received a premium of £5,500.

Expenditure on repairs, etc. incurred by Albert during the year ended 5 April 1997 were:

	£
Period to 30 June 1996	700
1 July to 29 September 1996	250
30 September 1996 to 5 April 1997	400

You are required to

1)   compute the income assessable under Schedule A for 1996/97; and

2)   compute the relief Jean can obtain in respect of the premium paid.

3.   CORELLI

Corelli, an unmarried man aged 41, owns three properties:

(A)   5 Arnhem Avenue;

(B)   17 Blenheim Road;

(C)   27 Cannae Road.

All are let out unfurnished.

(A)   This was let until 24 June 1996 at an annual rental of £1,200. On 29 September 1996, it was let out to a new tenant on a 10 year lease. The annual rental is £800. The tenant paid a premium of £5,000 on 29 September 1996.

(B)   This was let throughout 1996/97. The annual rental was £3,100. The rental due on 25 March 1997 was not received until 12 April 1996.

(C)   This was let from 24 June 1996 at an annual rental of £600.

All the rents are payable quarterly in advance on the normal quarter days and are sufficient normally to cover the landlord's outgoings.

Properties A and B were acquired in 1981; property C was purchased on 15 April 1996.

Expenditure in connection with the properties was as follows:

		A	B	C
Agent's commission	1.5.96	25	35	10
	1.11.96	25	35	10
Repairs (note)			100	1,800
Advertising for new tenants 10.7.96		50		

Note :

The repairs in respect of property C are analysed as follows:

	£
Installation of new kitchen equipment	300
Retiling part of the roof after damage in May 1996	1,500

Corelli's other income during 1996/97 was as follows:

	£
Dividends received	8,000
Salary	14,450

You are required to compute Corelli's tax borne for 1996/97.

4.   BENN

Benn, aged 38, is a married man. The following information is relevant for the year ended 5 April 1997:

(a)   his salary was £43,000

(b)   during the year he paid a personal pension contribution of £9,000 (gross value); no unused relief from earlier years is available

(c)   his other income was:

building society interest (net)   £240

dividends (including tax credit)   £80

(d)   since May 1994, he and his wife have had an investment account with the National Savings Bank in their joint names and the interest credited at 31 December was:

1994 - £200;   1995 - £280;   1996 - £260

(e)   in May 1997 Benn closed down a deposit account at the National Midbar Bank which he had kept for many years. Interest credited recently was:

	£
June 1995	40
December 1995	50
June 1996	51
December 1996	56
May 1997	20

(f)   his 8 year old daughter's dividends from a holding of shares he had gifted to her two years ago totalled £120 (including tax credit)

(g)   he paid allowable mortgage interest under MIRAS, of £3,095 (gross) and made covenanted payments of £386 (net of basic rate tax) to Oxfam under a four year deed executed in May 1993

(h)   his son, aged 10, has an income of £230 (gross) under a settlement made by his uncle

(i)   Benn cashed in his holding of the 25th issue of National Savings Certificates, receiving accumulated interest and a terminal bonus of £250

You are required to compute the tax borne by Benn for 1996/97.

5. BYRD LIMITED

You are a manager of Smith and Co, accountants, and the firm has recently been instructed to act as advisers to a newly incorporated manufacturing company, Byrd Ltd.

Mr Tallis, the managing director of Byrd Ltd, had requested you to write him a letter summarising the major points in the operation of a pay as you earn (PAYE) scheme in order that he can ensure his new book-keeper is operating the scheme correctly and maintaining the necessary records.

You have established that the staff complement comprises two full time working directors, one employee earning £8,400 per annum (plus substantial reimbursed expenses), the book-keeper earning £6,000 per annum and several part time employees each earning approximately £25 per week.

You are required to write a suitable letter from the firm to Mr Tallis, ensuring that your letter covers the following specific points:

1) requirements on employees joining and leaving;

2) records required for operation of PAYE and the completion of forms and returns;

3) calculation of pay and payment of monies to the Inland Revenue; and

4) end of year returns and forms.

Note: Ignore the requirements of the statutory sick pay scheme.

6. MR & MRS RUNDGREN

Rundgren and his wife separated permanently on 23 May 1996. On 1 August 1996 he agreed in writing to pay his wife maintenance of £3,000 (gross) per annum, payable in equal monthly amounts on the first of each month commencing with the date of the agreement. The Court later confirmed the allowance as part of their divorce proceedings, which also gave custody of their 15 year old daughter Bebe to Rundgren's wife.

Rundgren has for several years been employed as a travelling salesman for Utopia Limited. His salary had been £18,000 for the year to 30 June 1996 but on 1 July 1996 it was increased to £20,000 for the foreseeable future. Utopia's accounting year end is 31 December and in the May following bonuses are paid to star salesmen. Rundgren received the following amounts:

Year to 31 December 1995:	£7,250
Year to 31 December 1996:	£8,050
Year to 31 December 1997:	£8,750

Rundgren had PAYE of £7,200 deducted from his gross salary in 1996/97. In the same period he drove his company car 25,000 miles of which 16,000 related to business. The car has a 2,300 cc cylinder capacity and cost the company £15,000 two years ago. Rundgren paid the company £100 for private use of the car and £100 for the petrol he used when on holiday. Utopia Limited paid all other petrol bills.

To help him get over the trauma of the separation, Utopia Limited let Rundgren live rent-free in an investment property they had bought for £50,000 five years ago from 1 August 1996. The gross annual value of the house was £1,500. The company also paid his council tax charge for the year of £350 and a gas bill of £150 and bought furniture for £10,000.

The P11D form also showed 1996/97 BUPA subscriptions paid by Utopia Limited on Rundgren's behalf of £288. In December 1996 he had a minor operation which cost the scheme £212.

His wife was employed as an accountant by a menswear chain. To the date of separation she had received £2,000 (gross) from which PAYE had been deducted of £340 and for the rest of 1996/97 she received a gross salary of £10,000 (PAYE £1,700).

You are required to compute the income tax payable by, or repayable to, Mr Rundgren and Mrs Rundgren for the tax year 1996/97.

7.   MR & MRS BUNDY

Bundy, who is married and has one child, aged 5, has the following income:

	Year ended 5.4.96 £	Year ended 5.4.97 £
Salary as director of Walter & Walter Ltd	9,000	11,000
Income from property	150	175
Dividends (amounts received)	2,535	3,571
Interest on 3½% War Loan (acquired 1985)	24	24
Interest on new NSB ordinary account (opened May 1996)		136
His child's income comprised:		
Annuity under will of grandfather (gross)	360	360
Income from trust fund set up by Bundy in 1991 (gross)	200	250
Bundy made the following payments:		
Interest on building society mortgage (gross)	700	550
Contribution to approved superannuation fund (gross)	250	275
Mrs Bundy's income comprised:		
Salary as accountant	26,000	28,800
Dividends (amounts received)	1,188	1,549
Interest on building society deposit (net)	219	240

The mortgage interest was paid outside MIRAS on a loan of £8,000.

You are required to calculate the income tax borne by Mr Bundy and by Mrs Bundy for 1996/97. Assume they have made no election regarding their allowances.

8.   NORMAN

The tax returns of Norman, aged 45, show the following:

		Year ended 5 April 1996 £	Year ended 5 April 1997 £
Income			
	Salary and commission from Flyhigh Ltd	9,600	10,250
	Benefit in kind	240	350
	Rental income (net of expenses)	2,700	4,600
	Dividends - amounts received	5,349	6,400
Payments			
	Loan interest paid under MIRAS (gross)	Nil	3,924
	Maintenance to former wife (gross)	Nil	3,000
PAYE on salary		1,875	1,826

The loan interest is paid in respect of a mortgage of £36,000 on Norman's main residence, purchased in May 1996.

The maintenance to Norman's former wife was paid under a UK Court Order dated 31 March 1996.

On 9 October 1996 he married Hilda whose income for the year ended 5 April 1997 was:

	£
Earnings at £330 per month (PAYE £7 per month)	3,960
Building society interest - net amount credited 1 January 1997	160

You are required to compute:

1)   the tax payable by self assessment by Norman for 1996/97; and

2)   the repayment due to Hilda for 1996/97.

1.   MRS BUTCHER

Income tax repayment claim 1996/97	*Other income* £	*Savings income* £	*Tax suffered* £
State pension	3,180		
Occupational pension	4,900		1,133
Schedule A rent from cottage	977		
Schedule D Case III: 3¹/₂% War Loan £(355 + 355) ÷ 2		355	
National Savings Bank £((100 + 120) ÷ 2) - 70		40	
Dividends £240 x 100/80		300	60
Income element of annuity (net of tax @ 20%) (2,500 - 2,120)		380	76
Building society interest £4,000 x 100/80		5,000	1,000
	———	———	
STI (total £15,132)	9,057	6,075	
Age allowance	(4,910)		
	———	———	
Taxable income (total £10,222)	£4,147	£6,075	
	═══	═══	

	£
Tax suffered	£2,269
	═══

Income tax

			£
Lower rate band		£3,900 x 20%	780
Basic rate band:	other income	£247 x 24% £(4,147 - 3,900)	59
	savings income	£6,075 x 20%	1,215
			———
			2,054
Less tax reducer: APA £1,790 x 15%			(269)
			———
			1,785
Less tax suffered			(2,269)
			———
Repayment due			£(484)
			═══

2.   **ALBERT**

(a)   ALBERT SCHEDULE A ASSESSMENT 1996/97

	£	£	£
Lease of shop at full rent to Jim			
Rental: 3m to 30 June	600		
Less allowable repairs -			
period to 30.6.96	(700)	(100)	
Lease of shop at full rent to Jean			
Rental: 6m to 5 April	800		
Less allowable repairs			
1.7.96 to 29.9.96	(250)		
30.9.96 to 5.4.97	(400)	150	
			50
Lease premium paid by Jean			
Assessable lease premium			
- paid 29.9.96		5,500	
Less: 2% x (11 - 1) x £5,500		(1,100)	4,400
			£4,450

(b)   Jean will obtain a measure of income tax relief for the lease premium paid of £5,500 by treating the amount of the premium assessable on Albert of £4,400 as additional rent payable from day to day over the term of the lease and, as such, allowable in the computations of her trading income (at the rate of £400 per annum - £4,400/11).

3.   CORELLI

TAX BORNE COMPUTATION: 1996/97

	Other income £	Savings income £
Schedule E	14,450	
Dividends (£8,000 x 100/80)		10,000
Schedule A: rentals (W1)	2,460	
Schedule A: premium (W2)	4,100	
STI (total £31,010)	21,010	10,000
Less: PA	(3,765)	
Taxable income (total £27,245)	£17,245	£10,000

		£
Tax borne	£3,900 @ 20%	780
	£(17,245 - 3,900) = 13,345 @ 24%	3,203
	£(25,500 - 17,245) = 8,255 @ 20%	1,651
	£(10,000 - 8,255) = 1,745 @ 40%	698
	£27,245	£6,332

Workings

1. Schedule A assessment on rents

	A £	B £	C £
Income A £(1,200 x 3/12) + £(800 x 6/12)	700		
B		3,100	
C £(600 x 9/12)			450
Expenditure:			
Agents commission			
1.5.96	(25)	(35)	(10)
1.11.96	(25)	(35)	(10)
Repairs	-	(100)	(1,500)
Advertising	(50)	-	-
	£600	£2,930	£(1,070)
Net profits on Schedule A business		£2,460	

2. Schedule A assessment on lease premium

	£
Premium	5,000
Less: 2% x (10 - 1) x £5,000	(900)
Assessable under Schedule A	£4,100

4.   BENN

INCOME TAX 1996/97

	Other income £	Savings income £
Schedule E: salary	43,000	
Less: personal pension contributions (20% x £43,000) (max)	(8,600)	
	34,400	
Schedule D Case III		
NSB investment account - CYB £260 x ½		130
Bank interest - £(51 + 56) x 100/80		134
Building Society interest £240 x 100/80		300
Dividends		80
Daughter's dividends	120	
	34,520	
Less: covenanted payment £(386 x 100/76)	(508)	
STI (total £34,656)	34,012	644
Less: personal allowance	(3,765)	
Taxable income (total £30,891)	£30,247	£644

Tax borne

	£		£
	3,900	at 20%	780
	21,600	at 24%	5,184
	5,391	at 40%	2,156
	£30,891		8,120

Less: tax reducers		
Interest under MIRAS: ignore		
Married couple's allowance £1,790 x 15%		(269)
Tax borne		**£7,851**

Notes:

(1)   Income from National Savings Certificates is tax-free (s.46 ICTA 1988).

(2)   Child's income is treated as the parent's income if it arises from funds provided by the parent and exceeds £100 pa (s.660B ICTA 1988). The charge is under Sch D Case VI.

(3)   Income from property held jointly with a spouse is deemed to be shared equally unless the couple make the appropriate declaration of their actual beneficial interest. (s.282A ICTA 1988).

(4)   To find the tax liability we would have added the basic rate tax retained on the personal pension contributions and on the covenanted payment to the tax borne.

(5)   The excess personal pension contribution of £400 does not qualify for tax relief and must be returned.

5.   BYRD LIMITED

SMITH & CO
5 Ash Street, London, Wl

Ref: PI
T Tallis Esq
Byrd Ltd
2 Ivor Street
London W2

10 June 1996

Dear Sir,

Pay As You Earn (PAYE)

As requested we are writing to summarise the major points which require attention in operating the PAYE scheme for your staff.

If you have not already informed the Inland Revenue that you have recently taken on staff, you should ask your book-keeper to do so without delay to ensure a supply of suitable PAYE stationery and to avoid penalties for non-compliance with PAYE regulations. You will receive a PAYE guide from the Revenue.

Code Numbers

To operate PAYE correctly it is necessary to obtain an appropriate code number for each employee. The code number ensures that the employee is allocated the correct reliefs and deductions to which he is entitled prior to applying taxation to his taxable pay. When an employee joins the firm he should provide you with a form P45 which contains particulars of his code number, his pay and tax deducted so far in the current tax year. This form is prepared in three parts by the previous employer who has sent part 1 to the Inspector of Taxes. The new employee will hand parts 2 and 3 to you, as the new employer. You should then complete part 3 with details of the new employment, sends this part off to the tax office dealing with the company's PAYE affairs and retain part 2 in your permanent wages records. This allows the employee to be entered into the wages records for PAYE purposes as if he had been employed with your firm from the beginning of the tax year. Some employees may not have a form P45 (eg. school leavers). While uncoded they will suffer tax on their pay with only the benefit of minimal deductions. Such employees should complete a form P15 Coding Claim and send it to the Inland Revenue in order to obtain a correct coding which is issued on form P2. Employers are normally provided with a full supply of required stationery including forms P15.

Form P46

Where a new employee fails to produce a P45 certificate the new employer must send a form P46 to the Inspector of Taxes showing the employee's name, address and date on which employment started. The deduction procedure to be followed by the employer until the Inspector issues a notice of coding will depend on the certificate signed by the employee on the P46. If the employee certifies that this is the first employment after full-time education the emergency code prescribed by the Revenue is used on a cumulative basis. If the employee certifies that this is his only or main employment the emergency code is used on a non-cumulative or 'week one' basis. If the employee signs neither certificate the full lower/ basic rate of tax is deducted without taking account of any allowances.

Record keeping

A wages book should be maintained summarising the wages paid on each pay day and the wages to be paid to each employee should be calculated on a workings deduction sheet maintained for each employee.

The workings deduction sheet should be headed with standing information such as name, national insurance number, PAYE code operated etc. and there are spaces for calculation of the tax and national insurance deductions for each pay day in a tax year. On each pay day the gross wage is entered on the deduction sheet and added to the cumulative gross pay from the beginning of the tax year to the previous paydate. This will give the cumulative gross pay to date in the tax year. Tables supplied by the Inland Revenue are then referred to. The first are entitled 'Pay Adjustment Tables' and there is a table for each week and month in the tax year showing the proportion of the employee's tax free allowances (as shown by the employee's code) due to the pay date in the tax year. The free pay due is entered on the deduction sheet and deducted from the cumulative gross pay to date to give cumulative taxable pay to date in the tax year. Other tables supplied by the Inland Revenue are then referred to (taxable pay tables) which will show the cumulative tax due on the cumulative taxable pay and this figure is entered in the deduction sheet. The cumulative tax due to the previous pay date is deducted from this figure to give the tax due, or refundable, on this pay date.

NIC

National Insurance contributions (NIC) are calculated according to the gross pay paid on the pay date and not on the cumulative gross pay date in the tax year. Separate tables are supplied by the Inland Revenue showing the amount to be deducted from the employee's pay (the employee's contribution) and the amount the employer has to pay in addition to the employee's gross pay (the employer's contribution).

All tax and NIC due for pay days in a tax month (6th in one month to 5th in the tax month) should be paid to the Collector of Taxes within 14 days of the end of the tax month. If the payments to the Collector are likely to average less than £450 per month the payments can be made quarterly instead of monthly.

Records should be maintained of employees for whom no tax or NIC is due and all records should be kept for at least three years from the end of the tax year in which they relate as the Inland Revenue may wish to inspect them.

End of year procedures

At the end of each fiscal year (5 April) all deduction cards should be carefully checked to ensure that they have been accurately compiled. A summary of the deduction cards is prepared on a form P35 and any under or over payments in the year should be noted in the appropriate places on the form. The employer must declare a complete list of all employees for whom the employer was required to keep records in accordance with the PAYE regulations during the year, answer various questions which are designed to establish if the PAYE regulations have been complied with and what additional information will be supplied (eg. Forms P11D) and then sign that the form has been correctly completed. In the case of a company employer, the company secretary or a director must sign. The form P35 should be sent to the Inland Revenue on or before 19 May.

Any PAYE or NIC for the year which remains unpaid at 19 April will attract an interest charge from that date.

Directors

Forms P11D should also be prepared for all employees who are paid emoluments at the rate of £8,500 per annum or more. Emoluments include for this purpose reimbursement of expenses, without taking account of the fact that some of those expenses may ultimately be tax-deductible. For each director you will also need to complete a form P11D unless he works full time, does not earn at the rate of £8,500 per annum or more and does not hold more than 5% of the shares in the company. The form P11D will contain particulars of all benefits and reimbursed expenses provided for the employee concerned. A form P9D is required to show expense payments made to non-P11D employees apart from reimbursement of expenditure actually incurred in performance of duties. A further year end procedure is the preparation of forms P60 which are issued to all employees and which give details of total pay and tax deducted in the year. The form is completed on 3 part stationery, the other two parts being called Forms P14 which are for the Inland Revenue and DSS respectively.

The Inland Revenue is empowered to ask for various other returns and information which we have not detailed in this letter, but which we should be glad to expand upon if required. Please let us know if we can be of further assistance.

Yours faithfully,

Smith and Co.

6.   MR & MRS RUNDGREN

MR RUNDGREN - INCOME TAX COMPUTATION 1996/97

	£	£	£
Salary (1/4 x £18,000) + (3/4 x £20,000)			19,500
Bonus (received in 1996/97)			7,250
			26,750
Benefits in kind			
- car £15,000 x 35%	5,250		
- less: $1/3$ reduction for mileage	(1,750)		
- less contribution	(100)	3,400	
- petrol		1,320	
- medical insurance		288	5,008
			31,758
Accommodation			
- annual value (see note) (8/12 x £1,500)		1,000	
- council tax		350	
- gas bill		150	
- furniture ((20% x £10,000) x 8/12)		1,333	
			2,833
STI			34,591
Less: personal allowance			(3,765)
Taxable income			£30,826

Note: Since there is no indication that any of the three exempting situations apply, the benefit arising on the accommodation will be assessable.

	£		Tax £
First	3,900	@ 20%	780
Next	21,600	@ 24%	5,184
Next	5,326	@ 40%	2,130
	30,826		8,094

Less tax reducers		
Maintenance payments		
£3,000 x 9/12 = £2,250, limited to £1,790		
£1,790 x 15%	269	
Married couple's allowance £1,790 x 15%	269	
		(538)
Tax borne and tax payable		7,556
Less: tax already deducted under PAYE		(7,200)
Tax now due under self assessment		£356

MRS RUNDGREN - INCOME TAX COMPUTATION 1996/97

	£
Salary/STI	12,000
Less: personal allowance	(3,765)
Taxable income	**£8,235**

20% x	£3,900	780
24% x	£4,335	1,040
	£8,235	1,820

Less: tax reducer	
Additional personal allowance £1,790 x 15%	(269)
Tax borne and tax liability	1,551
Less: tax already deducted - PAYE (£1,700 + 340)	(2,040)
Tax repayable	£(489)

7. MR & MRS BUNDY

MR BUNDY & MRS BUNDY - INCOME TAX 1996/97

	Mr Bundy		Mrs Bundy	
	Other income £	Savings income £	Other income £	Savings income £
Salaries	11,000		28,800	
Less: superannuation	(275)			
	10,725			
Investment income				
Dividends (£3,571 x 100/80)		4,464		1,936
Schedule A		175		-
Schedule D III		24		-
NSB New source (136 - 70)		66		-
BSI (240 x 100/80)		-		300
Child's income Sch D VI	250			
STI (total £15,704/£31,036)	10,975	4,729	28,800	2,236
Less: personal allowance	(3,765)		(3,765)	
Taxable income (totals £11,939/£27,271)	£7,210	£4,729	£25,035	£2,236

		Mr Bundy £		Mrs Bundy £
Income tax				
£3,900 x 20%		780		780
£3,310 x 24% £(7,210 - 3,900)		794		
£4,729 x 20%		946		
£21,135 x 24% £(25,035 - 3,900)				5,072
£465 x 20% £(25,500 - 25,035)				93
£1,771 x 40% (£2,236 - 465)				708
		2,520		6,653
Less tax reducers				
Mortgage interest £550 x 15%		(83)		
Married couple's allowance £1,790 x 15%		(269)		
Tax borne		£2,168		£6,653

8. NORMAN

1)

NORMAN - INCOME TAX 1996/97

	Other income £	Savings income £
Schedule E:		
Salary & commission	10,250	
Benefit	350	
Schedule A rental income	4,600	
Dividends (£6,400 x 100/80)		8,000
STI (total £23,200)	15,200	8,000
Less: personal allowance	(3,765)	
Taxable income (total £19,435)	£11,435	£8,000

Tax payable		£
£3,900 x 20%		780
£7,535 x 24% £(11,435 - 3,900)		1,808
£8,000 x 20% (dividends)		1,600
		4,188
Less: tax reducers		
Interest under MIRAS: ignore		
Maintenance £1,790 x 15%	269	
Married couple's allowance £1,790 x 6/12 x 15%	134	
		(403)
Tax borne and tax liability		3,785
Less tax paid and suffered: PAYE	1,826	
dividends	1,600	
		(3,426)
Tax payable by self assessment		£359

2)   HILDA - INCOME TAX 1996/97

	Other income £	Savings income £
Schedule E	3,960	
Taxed interest (£160 x 100/80)		200
STI (total £4,160)	3,960	200
Less: personal allowance	(3,765)	
Taxable income (total £395)	£195	£200

		£
Tax payable		
£395 x 20%		79
Less tax paid and suffered: PAYE (£7 x 12)	84	
interest	40	
		(124)
Repayment due		£(45)